Toxic Leadership

Toxic Leadership: Research and Cases presents research and cases on toxic leadership that emerged from qualitative research on the followers of toxic leaders. The goal is to help students, researchers, and academics understand how toxic leadership emerges, how leaders can spot toxic leadership within their organizations, and discuss what they can do to stop toxic leaders from destroying organizational value.

The book pulls together various theories, models, and names (e.g., bad leadership, destructive leadership) for toxic leadership. The authors cover how power, culture, personality disorders, and followers contribute to the toxic leadership phenomenon. Readers will learn how toxic leaders impact organizations, the types of toxic leaders, signs of toxic leaders, and the environments they create. The authors share case studies for each toxic leader type to illustrate themes, coping strategies, and organizational outcomes. Each case is accompanied by a series of questions for reflection, study, and leadership development.

This book will be useful for students, researchers, and academics to help uncover signs of toxic leaders that are often hidden from upper management. It will also be helpful for leaders to develop organizational strategies and for followers to develop coping strategies.

Steven M. Walker holds a PhD degree in Leadership Studies from Gonzaga University in Spokane, Washington.

Daryl V. Watkins is an educator and US Navy Combat Veteran with a background in higher education, public transportation, information technology management, and military aviation.

Routledge Studies in Leadership Research

Digital Supply Chain Management
Reshaping Talent and Organizations
David B. Kurz and Muragan Anandarajan

Women Business Leaders
Identity, Resistance, and Alternative Forms of Knowledge in Saudi Arabia
Liela A. Jamjoom

Responsible Leadership in Corporate Governance
An Integrative Approach
Monique Cikaliuk, Ljiljana Eraković, Brad Jackson, Chris Noonan and Susan Watson

Leadership and China
Philosophy, Place and Practice
Edited by Ralph J Bathurst and Michelle Sitong Chen

Leadership and Narcissism in the Organization
Mateusz Grzesiak

Toxic Leadership
Research and Cases
Daryl V. Watkins and Steven M. Walker

Public Sector Leadership
A Human-Centred Approach
Petri Virtanen, Marika Tammeaid and Harri Jalonen

For more information about this series please visit: www.routledge.com/Routledge-Studies-in-Leadership-Research/book-series/RSLR

Toxic Leadership

Research and Cases

Steven M. Walker and Daryl V. Watkins

Routledge
Taylor & Francis Group
NEW YORK AND LONDON

First published 2023
by Routledge
605 Third Avenue, New York, NY 10158

and by Routledge
4 Park Square, Milton Park, Abingdon, Oxon, OX14 4RN

Routledge is an imprint of the Taylor & Francis Group, an informa business

Library of Congress Cataloging-in-Publication Data
Names: Walker, Steven, 1984– author. | Watkins, Daryl, 1965– author.
Title: Toxic leadership : research and cases / Steven Walker and Daryl Watkins.
Description: New York, NY : Routledge, 2023. | Includes bibliographical references and index.
Identifiers: LCCN 2022026560 | ISBN 9781032064611 (hardback) | ISBN 9781032064772 (paperback) | ISBN 9781003202462 (ebook)
Subjects: LCSH: Leadership—Moral and ethical aspects. | Business ethics. | Organizational behavior.
Classification: LCC HD57.7 .W339 2023 | DDC 658.4/092—dc23/eng/20220628
LC record available at https://lccn.loc.gov/2022026560

ISBN: 978-1-032-06461-1 (hbk)
ISBN: 978-1-032-06477-2 (pbk)
ISBN: 978-1-003-20246-2 (ebk)

DOI: 10.4324/9781003202462

Typeset in Bembo
by Apex CoVantage, LLC

Contents

Acknowledgments vii
Preface viii

1 Introduction 1

2 Toxic Leadership Definitions 7

3 Power 15

4 Personality Disorders 18

5 Followers 25

6 Culture 32

7 Model 42

8 Aberrant Behavior Cases 61

9 Abuse of Power Cases 74

10 Egocentric Cases 87

11 Emotional Dysregulation Cases 96

12 Ineffective Leadership Cases 106

13 Moral Corruption Cases 118

14 Coping Strategy Cases 128

15 Conclusion 136

Author Biographies 138
Index 140

Acknowledgments

The authors express their appreciation to everyone who directly or indirectly played a role in the development of this book. We want to thank the many people at Routledge, Taylor & Francis Group, especially Brianna Ascher, Naomi Round Cahalin, and Jessica Rech, for their support, encouragement, and gentle nudges toward the finish line.

We thank Dr. Nancy Watkins and Dr. Matthew Earnhardt for their input on the concepts and manuscript as they took shape. Their wisdom and counsel have made this a much better book.

We thank our families and friends for their patience in allowing us to be heads-down, writing and researching. We regret missing valuable time together.

Finally, we thank the oppressed followers who contributed their stories to this book. Without them, the cases in this book would not have taken shape.

Preface

Steven M. Walker

It is estimated that there were five million deaths in the 18th century due to war-related causes. In the 19th century, an estimated 20 million due to war-related causes. This past century, there were between 120 million and 150 million deaths due to war-related causes. Fifty million of those deaths are attributed to Mao Zedong. Twenty-three million deaths are attributed to Adlof Hitler. Twenty-seven million deaths are attributed to Joseph Stalin.

Three leaders.

Responsible for 100 million deaths.

That is the destructive power of leadership done the wrong way. That is the shadow side of leadership.

When teaching a subject such as leadership, I have always followed the pedagogical structure where one begins by examining and reflecting on each extreme. The shadow and light. First, one reflects on the darker sides of leadership, then one examines the light side. The first assignment of every course I teach on leadership requires the student to reflect on an experience with a toxic leader. The assignment requires no more than that. I don't like putting too many parameters around the assignment because I want the stories and reflections to be organic and real. Over the years, this has become my most popular assignment. While the essay only requires three pages in length, many students write double that number. There is no shortage of stories. These stories are dark, ruthless, unnerving, gut-wrenching, heartbreaking, and for me personally, a little too close to home. The stories resonated deeply because I had experienced similar ones myself. The unnerving part was that I had once considered these stories as just "normal" leadership stories.

Growing up, I never heard the term "toxic leader" unless it was used to describe one of the extreme examples shared above such as Hitler, Stalin, or Mao. However, there are examples of toxic leadership that, while perhaps unnoticed and not given much attention, can still cause deleterious long-term physical and psychological effects.

Toxic leadership was, in my experience, covered under the guise of "tough love", "pushing people to their limits", or the use of fear and coercion to influence followers to do what the leader and organization wanted. Greed was good. Competition and beating people down to get ahead was noble.

The turn of the century brought the Enron and WorldCom scandals, followed by more extreme and rampant corporate corruption and greed, eventually leading to the 2008 financial collapse and Great Recession. It was becoming clear that these toxic styles of leadership weren't just bad for the employees, but bad for overall organizational and economic sustainability. The fallout from the Great Recession of 2008 resulted in millions of people without jobs or places to live.

Unfortunately, things still haven't changed much.

But they need to change. They can change. Only we first need to acknowledge the problem. We must listen to the oppressed and provide them support. That is ultimately the mission of this book, to give a voice to the oppressed and by doing so, hopefully provide the oppressed some liberation, not only from acknowledging their pain, but learning from it and responding with change for the better.

Paulo Freire, a Brazilian educator and philosopher, argued that the role of a leader was to liberate, and to be liberated, with the people. He believed that the fundamental theme of this generation was that of *domination* – which implies it's opposite, the theme of liberation, as the objective to be achieved. This liberation was for both the oppressor and the oppressed.

I encourage you to read through this book with immense insight, goodwill, understanding, compassion, forgiveness, and love. You may find things that startle you, frustrate you, trigger you, and cause pain. You may even see parts of yourself in these pages. I know I do. And that is okay. Facing the shadow is how we heal and is the first step toward life-giving transformation. Let us start that healing and transformation together.

Dr. Steven M. Walker
San Diego, CA
May 15, 2022

Daryl V. Watkins

We are just on the tail end of escaping a global pandemic that has inexorably changed the organizational landscape. Organizations rapidly adapted to the pandemic by enabling remote work and relaxing previously sacrosanct oversight of employee movements. Working out of a cramped bedroom or a dining room table exposed many employees to the possibilities of a new way of working. As the pandemic ends, some organizations want to go back to business-as-usual. However, the lowest unemployment rate in decades has given employees agency to push for what they want. This newfound agency is atypical. Workers rarely feel empowered to push back against management. Indeed, most of the followers who contributed stories to this book did not push back. In some cases, the management-to-worker *imbalance of power* is so bad that workers feel they have to unionize to restore a reasonable amount of control.

My co-author, Steven, has been collecting these stories for a decade. I am grateful that he invited me to this project. The pandemic served as a temporal envelope around my deep dive into toxic leaders and toxic leadership. This exploration of toxic leadership, which started with two academic papers and culminates in this book, has been challenging. I am a positive person, typically looking to make the best of situations, to leave all things better than I found them. I prefer to study what makes us stronger. Toxic leaders keep us from being our best, doing great work, and using our strengths to chase our objectives.

Over the past year, the following conversation unfolded more times than I can remember!

Everyone: So, what have you been up to?
Me: I've been working on a book on toxic leaders.
Everyone: Toxic leaders? Oh my gosh! I have a story for you! Can I share my story with you?

Invariably, I ask people how they coped with their toxic leader. Usually, the answer is that people "sucked it up and stuck it out; I didn't know what to do." The odds seem stacked against standing up to a toxic boss for reasons we discuss in this book. Sometimes, they quit, reminding me of how I handled some of the toxic leaders in my life. Others were rescued from their version of Dante's inferno when their toxic bosses moved on to some promotion. There is an odd dilemma. Toxic leaders are so good at self-promotion that they often leave their positions for a promotion and a raise. But, more about that in the book.

We had three goals in writing this book:

1. Continue to shine a light on this subject to educate people about toxic leaders so that people know they are not alone
2. Share our model and typology of toxic leaders
3. Provide some relief by sharing some coping strategies and ways for organizations to think about and recognize toxic leaders.

The third goal is the noblest, and I hope that oppressed followers become empowered to stand up to the toxic leaders in their lives.

If this book resonates with you, please share a story about a toxic leader in your life at https://toxicleaderstory.com. Perhaps your story will end up in our next edition, and you will help make a difference for someone with a similar story. It can be incredibly liberating to (anonymously) take a load off your chest.

Fair Winds and Following Seas,

Dr. Daryl V. Watkins
Orange, CA
May 15, 2022

1 Introduction

Being a 911 dispatcher is a tough career. I average 200 phone calls in an eight-hour period. I answer a range of calls, such as from people drunk in public, kids being lost, car accidents, and even prank calls. I have a very stressful job. The absolute last thing I need is a direct supervisor that doesn't fairly supervise all the employees.

In 2007, I started dispatching for a new Sheriff's Department. I knew going into the job that the work conditions would be grueling. The station was undergoing a remodel, the city police department just merged with the Sheriff, and the city had a recent spike in crime. The dispatching room was relocated to a cramped office with no windows and barely enough room to accommodate all the 911 dispatchers. We were basically stuffed in a closet, answering priority calls back-to-back. My first call was about a deputy involved in a fight at a local bar. I was being yelled at by the witness on the 911 line, my co-dispatchers, and my supervisor, Deputy L.

Deputy L had been a supervisor of dispatchers for over ten years. She was known for her level-head and ability to bring out the best in her employees. If you were her favorite or her friend, it was great for you. If you fell on the other side, like I did and most others, good luck.

Deputy L openly criticized employees, not for their handling of the dispatch calls, but for the assignment of the calls to certain deputies in the field. She wanted her friends to get the easy calls and the deputies she wasn't friends with to get the more difficult calls. As dispatchers, you are trained to assign certain calls to trainees for them to gain experience and the rest are distributed to available deputies on duty. The way you gained L's favor was to bring her a Venti Chai Latte with Almond Milk at the beginning of the shift and that pretty much solidified your easy day as a patrol deputy. Deputy L would reassign radio calls to certain deputies after a dispatcher initially assigned them. She would yell out "reassign tag 212 to the rookie on the southside", knowing they were clear across town just so her friend didn't have to handle it.

Her behavior was very frustrating. She would invite her friends to extended lunches and cut our lunch short so we could handle the phones. Deputy L and her favorites would then return from these outings and discuss them at length while we are trying to handle emergent phone calls. The dispatch environment was a mess.

I can recall another incident when Deputy L was held over for an additional eight-hour shift and was told to draft two additional dispatchers. I was not next on

DOI: 10.4324/9781003202462-1

the rotational draft list and she did it anyway. Two other dispatchers volunteered to take my spot, but she refused and made me work. She knew I had plans that day and I was looking forward to it. She also knew that if I didn't comply, I could face disciplinary action. I held it together the entire shift. As I drove away with tears rolling down my face, I vowed to never speak again about my outside plans knowing that information could be used against me in the near future.

The environment around the dispatch room was thick with anxiety and stress. I always felt like I was walking on eggshells. We were never able to speak freely. Everyone did their best to avoid contact with Deputy L, as it was better to stay off her radar. You never knew when she was going to lash out or who would be her next victim of ridicule. As I think back over my time serving as a dispatcher there, I can feel my breathing being restricted. I started seeing a therapist as a result of me working that assignment.

After completing my one-year certification of 911 dispatcher, I began to look for other stations to work at for the Sheriff's Department. I went on seven different interviews. I prayed that some other station would pick me. Any place had to be better than where I was. During all those interviews, I knew I was doing a good job. I couldn't understand why I would get that follow-up call saying they didn't choose me. A few months later, I found out Deputy L was being contacted directly from all the stations I interviewed with. She would tell them that I wasn't reliable and that I wouldn't be a good fit at their unit. I was furious. However, I didn't want to confront her because it would have ended poorly for me. I went on another interview and finally got picked for the new assignment. I was overwhelmed with delight as I would finally be free of her toxicity. My last night was a Sunday, 10 p.m. to 6 a.m. It was a particularly busy night. The phones were ringing the entire shift. It was finally 6 a.m. and I was gathering my belongings to leave for my days off. As I turned to leave, Deputy L yelled out, "Smalls, you start your new assignment in two hours". I didn't believe her at all. She got her last jab at me. She then produced a folded-up paper that stated my release date was sent over ten days prior. I could do nothing but cry heavy tears all the way home.

Months after I left that assignment, I heard from several of my former co-dispatchers that they transferred to other stations. A new captain was assigned to the station, and he made a lot of changes. Deputy L was sent to Tactical Communications and Cultural Awareness training. She was also transferred to the field where she handled the kind of radio calls she used to reassign. She was never promoted to a rank above deputy and has since retired from the Sheriff's Department.

....

The preceding case illustrates what many followers face daily. Whether it is within an organization, at home, or in the community, stories like the one above are unfortunately commonplace within many organizations. Toxic work environments shaped with the help of toxic leaders can have damaging effects on the individual's mental and physical health, their careers, as well as the organization's productivity and bottom line.

Leadership has been a hot topic within the field of business and organizational effectiveness for decades. And for obvious reasons. Since business relationships are constantly developing in our globalized world, investigating the subject of leadership remains particularly important; thus, it is covered by scholars and academics worldwide (Daft, 2014; Hickman, 2010; Northouse, 2013). The reason is that leadership within an organization is one of the key ingredients for building a high-performance culture, which is, however, still elusive to many organizations (Anjum et al., 2018). Therefore, understanding how to implement a successful leadership strategy can be even more important than building successful technological, financial, and operational programs. On the other hand, dysfunctional and toxic leadership may affect the organization in the opposite way and, consequently, lead to negative organizational outcomes such as poor performance, low morale, and high turnover, which has significant financial implications. It is true that successful companies are successful due to various reasons; however, toxic leadership can be a predictor of organizational dysfunction (Anjum et al., 2018; Lipman-Blumen, 2004).

Over the decades, many leadership theories have been discussed. There seems to be no shortage on the research that examines the impact and contribution that positive leaders have made throughout the world. This research focuses on the good of leadership, what successful leadership is and should look like, the characteristics and styles of these positive leaders, and so on. But what about the bad and toxic leaders?

First, let's begin with what leadership *is*, the difference between the words "leader" and "leadership", and how we define each in this book.

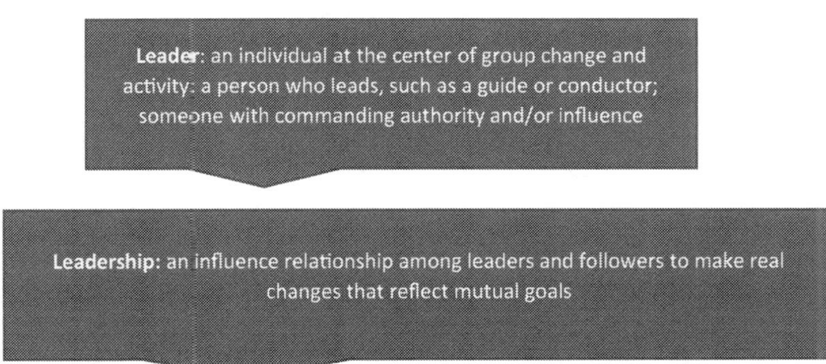

Figure 1.1 Definitions of leader and leadership

The conceptional definitions of a **leader** used for this text are Northouse's (2013) definition, which is "an individual at the center of group change and activity" (p. 5), and Merriam-Webster's dictionary definition "a person who leads, such as a guide or conductor; someone with commanding authority and/or *influence*". The conceptual definition of **leadership** used for this text is James Rost's (1993), which is "an *influence* relationship among leaders and followers to make real changes that reflect mutual goals".

There are numerous leadership theories and styles. Some of the more popular and well-known ones are the following:

Authoritative/autocratic: the leader dictates goals and has full control and power, leaving low autonomy for followers (Day & Hamblin, 1964).

Transformational: leader is a role model who inspires followers through idealized influence, inspirational motivation, individualized consideration, and intellectual stimulation (Burns, 2004).

Servant: leader's main goal is to serve those around him or her (Greenleaf, 2002).

Situational: leadership style used is dependent on the situation (Hersey, 1985).

Authentic: leader builds honest and open relationships and supports openness and transparency (Avolio & Gardner, 2005).

Adaptive: leadership that understands and works through change. These leaders tend to be both highly emotionally and contextually intelligent (Heifetz et al., 2009).

Leader–Member Exchange (LMX): The goal of LMX is to understand the effects of leadership on group members, team, and the overall organization. LMX claims that leaders form different relationships with different individuals and that strong relationships built on trust can be increased for the betterment of the whole. Since leaders hold different relationships with each individual, each individual will work differently based on their relationship with the leader (Graen & Uhl-Bien, 1995).

These are only a few of the numerous theories of leadership out there. However, these theories, while important, will not be the focus of this text. The subject of this text is on the darker and more toxic forms of leadership. Understanding the darker sides of our humanity can have transformational impacts on our personal leadership development. Understanding what *not to do* is just as important as understanding what *to do*.

Though we may have some ideas of what it takes to be a good leader, we have unfortunately experienced negative leaders, as well as their toxic leadership traits. These types of leaders attempt to create a culture in which they are the authority of the group, and the only purpose of their subordinates is to make their leader look good in front of their peers and superiors. We often wonder how these individuals were placed into leadership positions and how they were able to maintain that position. Toxic leadership can destroy the morale of the subordinates in the team and may cause an overall decrease in productivity within the organization (Kellerman, 2004; Lipman-Blumen, 2004; Tepper et al., 2006). Toxic leaders can also have insidious impacts on the overall physical and mental health of followers (Kellerman, 2004; Lipman-Blumen, 2004; Tepper et al., 2006).

While the topic of toxic leadership may seem straightforward to some, the authors have found this subject to be multilayered, complex, and dynamic. In this book we will explore the effects of diverse subjects such as power, mental disorders, culture, gender, race, personality, and followership and how they influence the toxic leader phenomenon.

The purpose of the book is to present a model of toxic leadership that emerged from qualitative research on the followers of toxic leaders. The goal is to help organizations understand how toxic leadership emerges, how leaders can spot toxic leadership within their organizations, and describe what they can do to stop toxic leaders from destroying organizational value. We also hope to give voice to the oppressed followers of toxic leaders who graciously shared their stories to help us prepare this manuscript. To accomplish this goal, case studies, discussion questions, and various other creative activities and assignments will be presented to help readers think critically and better understand, analyze, and approach the toxic leadership phenomenon in their day-to-day lives.

References

Anjum, A., Ming, X., Siddiqi, A. F., & Rasool, S. F. (2018, May 21). An empirical study analyzing job productivity in toxic workplace environments. *International Journal of Environmental Research and Public Health, 15*(5), 1035. https://doi.org/10.3390/ijerph15051035. PMID: 29883424; PMCID: PMC5982074.

Avolio, B. J., & Gardner, W. L. (2005). Authentic leadership development: Getting to the root of positive forms of leadership. *Leadership Quarterly, 16*, 315–338.

Burns, J. (2004). *Transformational leadership*. Grove Press. ISBN 9780802141187.

Daft, R. (2014). *The leadership experience*. Cengage Publishing.

Day, R. C., & Hamblin, R. L. (1964). Some effects of close and punitive styles of supervision. *American Journal of Sociology, 69*, 499–510.

Graen, G. B., & Uhl-Bien, M. (1995). Relationship-based approach to leadership: Development of leader–member exchange (LMX) theory of leadership over 25 years: Applying a multi-level multi-domain perspective. *The Leadership Quarterly, 6*(2), 219–247.

Greenleaf, R. (2002). *Servant leadership: A journey into the nature of legitimate power and greatness*. Paulist Press.

Heifetz, R. A., Linsky, M., & Grashow, A. (2009). *The practice of adaptive leadership*. Harvard Business Press.

Hersey, P. (1985). *The situational leader*. Warner Books. ISBN:978-0446513425.

Hickman, G. (2010). *Leading organizations: Perspectives for a new era* (2nd ed.). Sage.

Kellerman, B. (2004). *Bad leadership: What it is, how it happens, why it matters*. Harvard Business School Publishing.

Lipman-Blumen, J. (2004). *The allure of toxic leaders: Why we follow destructive bosses and corrupt politicians-and how we can survive them*. Oxford University Press.

Northouse, P. (2013). *Leadership theory and practice* (6th ed.). Sage Publications Inc.

Rost, J. (1993). *Leadership for the 21st century*. Praeger Publishing.

Tepper, B., Duffy, M., Henle, C., & Lambert, L. (2006). Procedural injustice, victim precipitation, and abusive supervision. *Personnel Psychology*, *59*, 101–123.

2 Toxic Leadership Definitions

The term ***toxic leader*** was originally made popular by the American political scientist Dr. Marcia Whicker (1996), who referred to these types of leaders as bullies, fighters, malicious, maladjusted, and who enjoy tearing others down rather than uplifting their followers. Several years later, in the wake of high-profile ethical scandals such as Enron and WorldCom, toxic leadership became a topic area of interest once again as scholars began to question the role leaders played in these destructive organizational outcomes (Kellerman, 2004; Lipman-Blumen, 2004; Tepper, 2007).

According to Lipman-Blumen (2004), toxic leadership was "a process in which leaders, by dint of their destructive behavior and/or dysfunctional personal characteristics, inflict serious and enduring harm on their followers, their organizations, and non-followers, alike" (p. 36). Lipman-Blumen (2004) went on to describe ***toxic leadership*** as having the effect of a poison on their followers. Lipman-Blumen defined this type of leader as one who lacks self-control, is uncaring or unkind, and ignores the needs, wants, and wishes of their followers (as cited in Hickman, 2010, p. 397). Additionally, toxic leadership has also been described as inflicting intense and lasting damage by exhibiting destructive behaviors and other dysfunctional personal qualities to those they intend to control, as well as others who may be indirectly impacted (Lipman-Blumen, 2004, p. 19). The behaviors or personal characteristics "must inflict some reasonably serious and enduring harm on their followers and their organizations" (p. 19). The label of "seriously toxic leaders" is reserved for those who act with an intent to harm or to enhance the self at the expense of others, since some toxic leaders are blissfully unaware of how their incompetence hurts their subordinates and organizations (p. 20). Toxic leaders manipulate, oppress, deceive, and incompetently lead with ego and imprudent ambition (Lipman-Blumen, 2004). The result of these behaviors could cause irreversible harm to the team and to the organizational culture, as staff may become disenchanted with their roles and become hostile, which is easily transmitted to other staff (Lipman-Blumen, 2004).

Reed (2004) also discussed toxic leadership, referring to it as a *syndrome*. The toxic leader syndrome, according to Reed (2004), included three primary things: lack of concern for followers, a personality and/or interpersonal

DOI: 10.4324/9781003202462-2

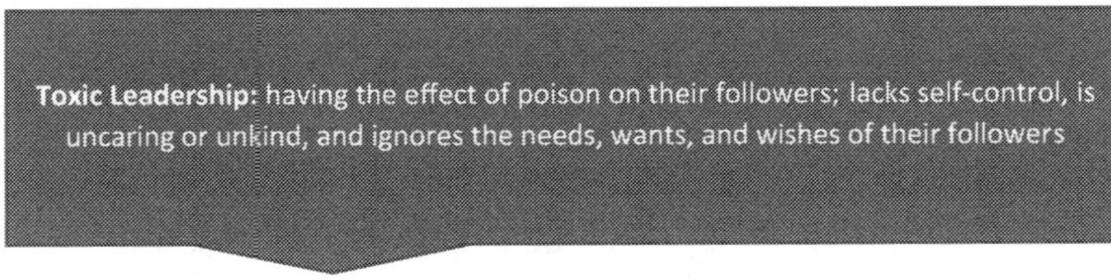

Figure 2.1 Definition of toxic leadership

behaviors that harms the organizational culture, and is motivated by self-interest (pp. 6–7). Overall, toxic leaders will tear others down to build themselves up and appear as a strong leader. These individuals are usually appointed for appearing to be knowledgeable in their job and appearing to have good relationships with others. In reality, they delegate their work to their subordinates, hijack their follower's ideas, and disguise them as their own, and if an issue arises in the process, they will designate a scapegoat in order to avoid appearing wrong or incompetent.

And finally, Steele (2011) added to the discussion by arguing that toxic leaders can still be effective in their mission or completion of organizational objectives, despite their toxicity. However, mission effectiveness and goal completion do not mean positive outcomes for followers. Steele (2011) contended that these toxic leaders can be strong leaders, but it is their innate desire to self-promote above all else that makes them toxic.

Destructive Leadership

Another term frequently used in the literature to describe toxic leadership is **destructive leadership** (Einarsen et al., 2007; Krasikova et al., 2013; Pelletier, 2010; Tepper, 2007). Einarsen et al. (2007) defined destructive leadership as the "systematic and repeated behavior by a leader, supervisor, or manager that violates the legitimate interest of the organization by undermining and/or sabotaging the organization's goals, tasks, resources, and effectiveness and/or motivation, well-being or job satisfaction of subordinates" (p. 208). For Pelletier (2010), destructive leadership includes both physical force such as sexual harassment and physical assault, as well as passive behavior such as failing to provide feedback or supporting the followers (p. 375).

Krasikova et al. (2013) defined destructive leadership as

> *volitional behavior by a leader that can harm or intends to harm a leader's organization and/or followers by (a) encouraging followers to pursue goals that contravene the legitimate interests of the organization and/or (b) employing a leadership style that involves the use of harmful methods of influence with followers, regardless of justifications for such behavior.*
>
> (p. 1310)

> **Destructive Leadership:** systematic and repeated behavior by a leader, supervisor, or manager that violates the legitimate interest of the organization by undermining and/or sabotaging the organization's goals, tasks, resources, and effectiveness and/or motivation, well-being or job satisfaction of subordinates

Figure 2.2 Definition of destructive leadership

To summarize more succinctly, Krasikova et al. (2013) contended that destructive leadership is "harmful behavior embedded in the process of leading" (p. 1310). For Krasikova et al. (2013), destructive leadership is *intended* harm to the organization or followers. This is different from leadership that is ineffective, where the leader is incompetent and therefore harms the organization and its followers through a lack of experience or knowledge. Per Krasikova et al.'s definition, there are two ways in which destructive leadership can manifest itself: encouraging followers to pursue destructive goals and using destructive methods to influence and coerce followers (p. 1311).

For Schyns and Schilling (2013), destructive leadership encompasses only follower-targeted influence rather than destructive leader behaviors that are not related to tasks or goals of the organization (p. 139). Schyns and Schilling (2013) therefore define destructive leadership as "a process in which over a longer period of time the activities, experiences and/or relationships of an individual or the members of a group are repeatedly influenced by their supervisor in a way that is perceived as hostile and/or obstructive" (p. 141). Similarly to Krasikova et al. (2013), Schyns and Schilling (2013) do not include leadership that is ineffective or incompetent in their definition of destructive leadership. For these authors, the destructive leadership should not be defined by the outcomes and consequences but rather on the destructive behaviors of a leader targeted specifically at the followers (Krasikova et al., 2013; Schyns & Schilling, 2013).

Bad Leadership

Kellerman (2004), one of the first to pioneer research into ***bad leadership***, contended that bad leadership fell into two categories: ineffective and unethical. Ineffective leaders were ones that failed to produce desired outcomes and fell short of organizational objectives due to their missing traits, weak skills, or poorly employed tactics. Unethical leaders, on the other hand, were ones that failed to distinguish between right and wrong, did not exercise their leadership for the common good, and put their own needs before others. Kellerman (2004) went on to break down these two categories of bad leaders into seven groups:

- **Incompetent** – "the leader and at least some followers lack the will or skill (or both) to sustain effective action. With regard to at least one leadership challenge, they do not create positive change" (p. 34).
- **Rigid** – "the leader and at least some followers are stiff and unyielding. Although they may be competent, they are unable or unwilling to adapt to new ideas, new information, or changing times" (p. 34).
- **Intemperate** – "the leader lacks self-control and is aided and abetted by followers who are unwilling or unable to intervene" (p. 35).
- **Callous** – "the leader and at least some followers are uncaring and unkind. Ignored or discounted are the needs, wants, and wishes of most members of the group or organization, especially subordinates" (35).
- **Corrupt** – "the leader and at least some followers lie, cheat, and steal. To a degree that exceeds the norm, they put self-interest ahead of the public interest" (p. 36).
- **Insular** – "the leader and at least some followers minimize or disregard the health and welfare of 'the other' – that is, those outside the group or organization for which they are responsible" (p. 36).
- **Evil** – "the leader and at least some followers commit atrocities. They use pain as an instrument of power. The harm done to others is severe rather than slight. The harm can be either physical, psychological, or both" (p. 37).

Similar to Kellerman (2004), Fors Brandebo et al. (2016) consider outcomes and consequences as vital elements to be included in the formula of bad leadership. "If the outcomes of leadership are destructive for the organization and/or the subordinates, the behavior should be regarded as destructive regardless of the cause (inefficiency, etc.) or intention, especially if the behavior is repeated and systematic" (Fors Brandebo et al., 2016, p. 692).

In contrast, Roque et al. (2020) add a more ethical and moral stance to the definition of bad leadership. For Roque et al. (2020), bad leadership is defined more by the unethical cultures that the leader creates within the organization, more so than the specific behaviors of the leader.

> Leaders have an enormous influence in the creation and support of an ethical culture and intrinsically also in its destruction: "A single change in top management can also have a significant negative impact on ethical corporate cultures" (Schwartz, 2013, p. 47). More than that, in some cases, "it only takes one bad leader to bring down an organization" (Boddy et al., 2010, p. 125).
>
> (Roque et al., 2020, p. 276)

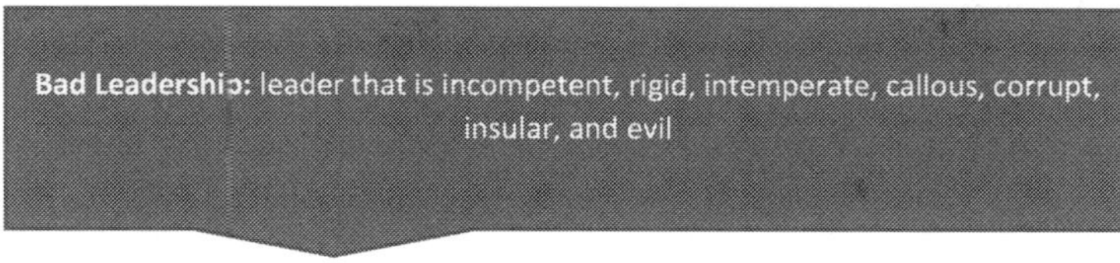

Figure 2.3 Definition of bad leadership

Additionally, Conrad and Nash (2013) define bad leadership as leadership that influences through command-and-control techniques rather than by example. Similarly, Fors Brandebo et al. (2016), Kellerman (2004), and Roque et al. (2020), Conrad and Nash (2013) argue that outcomes and consequences should be considered within the definition of bad leadership. Conrad and Nash (2013) point out the negative impact bad leadership can have on follower performance and mental health, as well as the erosion of productivity that bad leadership brings to the organization. In summary, there appears to be no solid and universally agreed-upon definition of "bad leadership". Per the literature, bad leadership appears to be an influence relationship that brings with it deleterious effects across the organizational spectrum.

Bullying

Einarsen (2003) defined ***bullying*** as harassing and offensive behavior that negatively affects someone's work. In addition to this definition, Einarsen (2003) contended that the bullying had to happen repeatedly and regularly over a period of time. Pelletier (2010) later added that bullying required one to use their mental or physical strength against a weaker individual or an individual in a lower position than themselves. Hoel et al. (2001) described bullying as a condition where vulnerable targets are treated with hostile behavior over a long period of time. The targeted individuals then have a difficult time defending themselves against this hostile behavior.

Within the literature, the topic and definition of workplace bullying evolved to link both directly and indirectly to the leader. Directly in that the leader themselves are the ones bullying followers (Plonien, 2016), and indirectly where the organizational climate that the leader creates increases the risk of bullying between employees (Nielsen, 2013). Bullying from a leader is described by Plonien (2016) as abusive behavior in the form of yelling, throwing things, and publicly belittling and embarrassing followers (p. 108). Similarly, Nielsen (2013) defined bullying as

> a situation where one or several individuals persistently, and over a period of time, perceive themselves to be on the receiving end of

> negative actions from superiors or co-workers, and where the target of the bullying finds it difficult to defend him or herself against these actions.
>
> (p. 127)

Bullying that takes place within the department between followers, rather than between the leader and the follower, is described as arrogance and blatant disrespect for each other that can take the form of verbal abuse (p. 109). Plonien (2016) contended that transactional styles of leadership along with rigid and hierarchical organizational structures are partially responsible for creating climates where bullying can occur. Additionally, the more power that a leader holds, the more likely the bullying will continue without correction (p. 108).

Nielsen (2013) found that the laissez-faire leadership style can create organizational climates where bullying behavior among followers can flourish. Laissez-faire leadership is also known as inactive or ineffective leadership. Laissez-faire leadership happens when the individual with positional power refuses to lead and is mostly inactive and absent. According to Nielsen (2013), this style of leadership fosters "frustration and stress within the work group, which may also result in interpersonal tensions, escalated conflict levels and anti-social behavior such as workplace bullying" (p. 128).

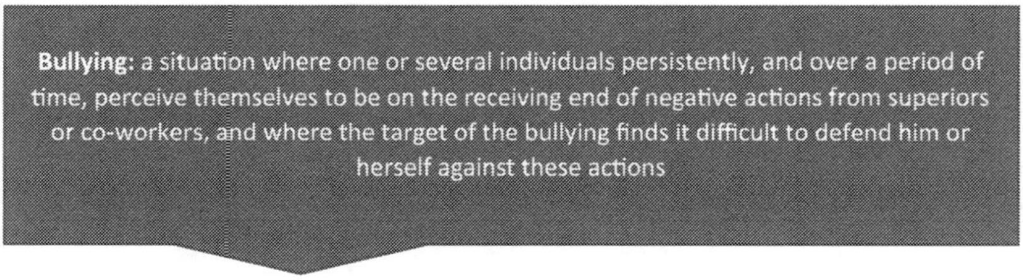

Figure 2.4 Definition of bullying

Table 2.1 Toxic Leadership Typology

Type	*Characteristics*	*References*
Toxic leadership	Uncaring, unkind, causes harm to followers and organizations, ego-driven, deceitful, oppressive, manipulative	Lipman-Blumen (2004) Reed (2004) Steele (2011)
Destructive leadership	Intended harmful behavior, pursuing destructive goals	Pelletier (2010) Krasikova et al. (2013), Schyns and Schilling (2013)

Type	Characteristics	References
Dark or shadow leadership (linked to psychological and personality disorders)	Psychopathy, narcissism, Machiavellianism	Khoo and Burch (2008), Mathieu et al. (2014), de Haan (2016), Fisher et al. (2010)
Bad leadership	Ineffective, incompetent, unethical, rigid, intemperate, callous, corrupt, insular, evil	Kellerman (2004), Fors Brandebo et al. (2016), Roque et al. (2020), Conrad and Nash (2013)
Bullying	Belittling, yelling, disrespect, arrogance	Einarsen (2003) Hoel et al. (2001)

References

Conrad, D., & Nash, S. (2013). Learning from bad leadership: MBA students reflect on bad leadership and lessons learned. *International Journal of Business and Social Research, 2*, 6.

de Haan, E. (2016) The leadership shadow: How to recognize and avoid derailment, hubris and overdrive. *Leadership (London, England), 12*(4), 504–512. https://doi.org/10.1177/1742715015572526

Einarsen, S. (2003). *Bullying and emotional abuse in the workplace: International perspectives in research and practice*. Taylor & Francis.

Einarsen, S., Aasland, M. S., & Skogstad, A. (2007). Destructive leadership behavior: A definition and conceptual model. *The Leadership Quarterly, 18*, 207–216.

Fisher, K., Hutchings, K., & Sarros, J. (2010). The "bright" and "shadow" aspects of in extremis leadership. *Military Psychology, 22*(S1), S89–S116. https://doi.org/10.1080/08995601003644346

Fors Brandebo, M., Nilsson, S., & Larsson, G. (2016). Leadership: Is bad stronger than good? *Leadership & Organization Development Journal, 37*(6), 690–710. https://doi.org/10.1108/LODJ-09-2014-0191

Hickman, G. (2010) *Leading organizations: Perspectives for a new era* (2nd ed.). Sage.

Hoel, H., Cooper, C. L., & Faragher, B. (2001). The experience of bullying in Great Britain: The impact of organizational status. *European Journal of Work and Organizational Psychology, 10*, 443–465.

Kellerman, B. (2004). *Bad leadership: What it is, how it happens, why it matters*. Harvard Business School Publishing.

Khoo, H., & Burch, G. (2008). The "dark side" of leadership personality and transformational leadership: An exploratory study. *Personality and Individual Differences, 44*(1), 86–97. https://doi.org/10.1016/j.paid.2007.07.018

Krasikova, D. V., Green, S. G., & LeBreton, J. M. (2013). Destructive leadership: A theoretical review, integration, and future research agenda. *Journal of Management, 39*(5), 1308–1338. https://doi.org/10.1177/0149206312471388

Lipman-Blumen, J. (2004). *The allure of toxic leaders: Why we follow destructive bosses and corrupt politicians-and how we can survive them*. Oxford University Press.

Mathieu, C., Neumann, C., Hare, R., & Babiak, P. (2014). A dark side of leadership: Corporate psychopathy and its influence on employee well-being and job satisfaction. *Personality and Individual Differences*, *59*, 83–88. https://doi.org/10.1016/j.paid.2013.11.010

Nielsen, M. B. (2013). Bullying in work groups: The impact of leadership: Bullying in work groups. *Scandinavian Journal of Psychology*, *54*(2), 127–136. https://doi.org/10.1111/sjop.12011

Pelletier, K. L. (2010). Leader toxicity: An empirical investigation of toxic behavior and rhetoric. *Leadership*. *6*(4), 373–389.

Plonien, C. (2016). Bullying in the workplace: A leadership perspective: Perioperative leadership. *AORN Journal*, *103*(1), 107–110. https://doi.org/10.1016/j.aorn.2015.11.014

Reed, G. E. (2004, July–August). Toxic leadership. *Military Review*, 67–71.

Roque, Moreira, J. M., Dias Figueiredo, J., Albuquerque, R., & Gonçalves, H. (2020). Ethics beyond leadership: Can ethics survive bad leadership? *Journal of Global Responsibility*, *11*(3), 275–294. https://doi.org/10.1108/JGR-06-2019-0065

Schyns, & Schilling, J. (2013). How bad are the effects of bad leaders? A meta-analysis of destructive leadership and its outcomes. *The Leadership Quarterly*, *24*(1), 138–158. https://doi.org/10 1016/j.leaqua.2012.09.001

Steele, J. P. (2011, June). Antecedents and consequences of toxic leadership in the U.S. Army: A two-year review and recommended solutions. *Center for Army Leadership*, 1–37.

Tepper, B. (2007). Abusive supervision in work organizations: Review synthesis, and research agenda. *Journal of Management*, *33*, 261–289.

Whicker, M. (1996). *Toxic leaders: When organizations go bad*. Quorum Books. ISBN:9780899309989.

3 Power

An important dynamic to consider when discussing the topic of toxic leadership is that of power. One of the characteristics of toxic leaders is the abuse of their power and the oppression this abuse of power causes among their followers. Power is defined as "the ability to influence the behavior of others to get the outcome you want" (Lewicki et al., 2015, p. 4). There are two primary types of power: soft power and hard power. Soft power is defined as influence through trust and relationships (Lewicki et al., 2015). Hard power is defined as influence through coercion, force, or threats (Lewicki et al., 2015).

A leader's soft power rests on three things primarily: the culture they help create, the values the leader represents, and the policies the leader enacts (Northouse, 2013). These things can create a perception by others that the leader has legitimate moral authority. Soft power takes time to create, build, and sustain not only the reputation needed to successfully wield power, but to build up the foundational relationships as well. Hard power is used when time is limited, action needs to be taken immediately, and you know you don't have the ability to wield soft power with the other party (Northouse, 2013).

According to Northouse (2013), there are five primary bases of power. The first is coercive power, which is conveyed through the fear of losing one's job, being demoted, or having things taken away. This power is gained by threatening others. The second base of power is reward power. This type

Power: the ability to influence the behavior of others to get the outcome you want

Soft Power: influence through trust and relationships

Hard Power: influence through coercion, force, or threats

Figure 3.1 Definitions of power, soft power, and hard power

DOI: 10.4324/9781003202462-3

of power is gained by the leader's ability to give something such as money, raises, or bonuses. The third base of power is referred to as legitimate power or positional power. The fourth base of power is expert power, which is gained through one's experience, skill, or knowledge of something. The fifth and final primary base of power is referent power, or the power gained from trust and respect of the leader or the leader's overall charisma.

The dynamics of power could be seen as a relational concern within the leader and follower relationship (Northouse, 2013, p. 11). Northouse argued that the base of power that can lead to toxicity within the leadership phenomenon is that of coercive power.

> To coerce means to influence others to do something against their will and may include manipulating penalties and rewards in their work environment. Coercion involves the use of threats, punishments, and negative rewards. Classic examples of coercive leaders are Adolf Hitler in Germany, the Taliban leaders in Afghanistan, Jim Jones in Guyana, and North Korea's Kim Jong-Un, each of whom has used power and restraint to force followers to engage in extreme behaviors.
>
> (p. 11)

Leaders who wield coercive power are only interested in their own personal gain and goals. This runs against the ideal forms of leadership where the leader is one who works *with* the followers to achieve a common goal.

Biological Influences of Power

Dominance hierarchy is a term used by biologists very regularly because almost all animal species that compete for occupation of a specific territorial space tend to organize themselves into fairly predictable hierarchies. Some authors have even claimed it to be a biological universal (De Waal, 2007). The neural biological systems that *Homo sapiens* evolved to deal with dominance hierarchy placement are at least one-third of a billion years old. For reference there weren't trees one-third of a billion years ago.

De Waal (2007), a Dutch primatologist, extensively researched the emergence of morality in chimpanzees. One of the things De Waal noted was that in chimpanzee hierarchies the brutal males that exercised coercive power did have the ability rise to the top leadership position within the group, but these coercive chimps tended to have very short-lived empires and to meet very violent deaths. De Waal (2007) concluded that for a chimpanzee hierarchy to be sustainable across time, the top chimp leader had to be quite pro-social. This meant that the chimp leader had to engage in sufficient reciprocal behavior, which allowed the leader to create and sustain relationships and allies within the group. On the other hand, if you were chimp leader and you had established your dominance merely as a matter of intimidation and strength, then the other chimps would be waiting for you to have an off day so they could take you down.

De Waal (2007) contended that stable chimp troop leaders had strong friendships, tended to treat the females well (by chimp standards), and paid a fair amount of attention to the infants. What these findings indicate from a perspective of power is that at a level that's below the human there's an ethic associated with leadership that isn't a mere consequence of raw coercive power and the abuse of power. Could this perhaps be similar to the power that leaders choose to utilize with their followers and whether or not the use of that power is effective and sustainable over time?

References

De Waal, F. (2007). *Chimpanzee politics: Power and sex among apes.* Johns Hopkins University Press.

Lewicki, R. J., Barry, B., & Saunders, D. M. (2015). *Negotiation, readings, exercises, and cases* (7th ed.). McGraw-Hill. ISBN:978-0-07-786242-8

Northouse, P. (2013). *Leadership theory and practice* (6th ed.). Sage.

4 Personality Disorders

Some researchers have titled these negative leadership behaviors and characteristics under different terms. Researchers such as Khoo and Burch (2008), for example, have referred to these dysfunctional workplace dispositions as ***dark leadership***. For Khoo and Burch (2008), dark leadership is mostly narcissistic. Similarly, Mathieu et al. (2014) defined dark leadership as those leaders that held the ***dark triad of personality*** (psychopathy, narcissism, Machiavellianism). Dark leadership created similar experiences for both the followers and the organizational culture. Under the control of dark leadership, followers reported such things as psychological distress, low job satisfaction and morale, and high family–work conflict (Mathieu et al., 2014).

Another term used to reference dysfunctional leadership is shadow leadership or the shadow side of leadership (de Haan, 2016; Fisher et al., 2010; Nigro, 2018). Characteristics of these shadow leaders were mentioned as aggressive behavior and corrupt or unethical decision-making, which resulted in organizational environments with high stress (Fisher et al., 2010). These characteristics found by Fisher et al. (2010) were somewhat different from the definitions and explanations given for dark leadership. However, for Nigro (2018), the description of shadow leadership was nearly identical to those for dark leadership. For Nigro (2018), shadow leadership consisted of "psychopathy, narcissism, Machiavellianism, and sadism" (p. 97), resulting in poor team performance.

Hogan and Hogan (2001) argued the reason for these dark or shadow leadership traits could be linked to the personality disorder of the leader. Hogan and Kaiser (2005) extended the model to suggest that personality directly determines leadership style, which in turn affects employee attitudes and team functioning and ultimately organizational performance.

According to Goldman (2009), there are four personality disorders that are linked to toxic leadership: paranoid personality disorder, anti-social personality disorder, borderline personality disorder, and narcissistic personality disorder. A mental diagnosis, such as personality disorder, is a clinical assessment of an individual by a trained professional such as a therapist, counselor, or psychiatrist. *The Diagnostic and Statistical Manual of Mental Disorders* (DSM) is

DOI: 10.4324/9781003202462-4

the primary manual for diagnosing mental disorders and the primary clinical source for mental illness in the United States.

According to the American Psychiatric Association (American Psychiatric Press, 2000), a personality disorder is defined in the DSM-V-TR as the following:

> A personality disorder is an enduring pattern of inner experience and behavior that deviates from the standards and expectations of the individual's culture. Personality disorders occur during adolescence or the early adulthood stages of life and are not limited to one specific gender. They are stable over time and lead to distress or impairment of the affected individual. This will hamper an individual to successfully function in a social or occupational setting.
>
> (p. 689)

A mental illness diagnosis for anyone should be done only by qualified professionals. Individuals with personality disorders demonstrate behaviors that deviate from common societal and organizational norms that the individual lives under. Individuals diagnosed with personality disorder will act out in unique ways within an organization. While some individuals diagnosed with personality disorder can be agreeable and compassionate, others can be pessimistic, manipulative, and egocentric (Kapuchinski, 2007). When the individual is confronted by their superiors regarding this behavior, the individual will blame others for their mistakes rather than take responsibility (Kapuchinski, 2007).

Paranoid Personality Disorder

The American Psychiatric Association (American Psychiatric Press, 2000) defined the paranoid personality disorder in the DSM-V-TR as the following:

> Individuals who suffer from this disorder have a repeated pattern of pervasive distrust and suspiciousness of others, beginning by early adulthood and present in a variety of contexts, as indicated by four (or more) of the following: (a) Suspects, without sufficient basis, believe that others are exploiting, harming, or deceiving him or her. (b) They are preoccupied with unjustified doubts about loyalty or trustworthiness of friends and associates. (c) They are reluctant to confide in others because they believe information given will be used against them at a later date. (d) They read hidden demeaning or threatening meanings into benign remarks or events. (e) They persistently bear grudges, unforgiving of insults, injuries, or sights. (f) They perceive that attacks on his or her character or reputation that are not apparent to others and are quick to react angrily or to counterattack. (g) Paranoid individuals

> have recurrent suspicions, without justification, regarding fidelity of spouse or sexual partner.
>
> (p. 694)

Paranoid personality disorder is found mostly in men and accounts for as much as 2.5% of the US population. According to Lubit (2004), the toxic traits of individuals suffering from paranoid personality disorder can be arrogance, poor communication, and blaming others for their mistakes (p. 55).

Anti-Social Personality Disorder

The American Psychiatric Association (2000) defined the anti-social personality disorder in the DSM-V-TR as the following:

> Individuals who are diagnosed with the Antisocial Personality disorder have three or more of the following. (a) They may repeatedly perform acts that are grounds for arrest (whether they are arrested or not) such as destroying property, harassing others, stealing, or pursuing illegal activities. Those who suffer from the Anti-social Personality Disorder have other characteristics that define their behavior. (b) They are very deceitful, as indicated by repeatedly lying, use of aliases, or conning others for personal profit or pleasure. (c) They are very impulsive and fail to plan. (d) They are irritable and aggressive, as indicated by repeated physical fights or assaults. (e) They have the reckless disregards for others. (f) They are consistently irresponsible, as indicated by the repeated failure to sustain consistent work behavior or honour financial obligations. (g) They show a lack of remorse, as indicated by being indifferent to or rationalizing having hurt, mistreated, or stolen from another.
>
> (p. 706)

Anti-social personality disorder is found in up to 3% of men and 1% of women in the United States. Individuals with anti-social personality disorder are typically intelligent and charismatic and can use their intelligence and charisma to influence their followers at first. These individuals may also be referred to as psychopaths or sociopaths in that they will use their influence to control and manipulate others. Toxic traits of individuals suffering from anti-social personality disorder include immoral and unethical behavior, manipulation, and threatening and bullying others (Lubit, 2004).

Borderline Personality Disorder

The American Psychiatric Association (2000) defined the borderline personality disorder in the DSM-V-TR as the following:

> The essential feature of Borderline Personality Disorder is a pervasive pattern of instability of interpersonal relationships, self-image, and

> affects, and marked impulsivity that begins by early adulthood and is present in a variety of contexts, as indicated by five (or more) of the following: (a) These individuals have frantic efforts to avoid real or imagined abandonment. (b) They have a pattern of unstable and intense interpersonal relationships characterized by alternating between the extremes of idealization and devaluation. (c) They have an identity disturbance, marked and persistent unstable self-image or sense of self. (d) They are impulsive in at least two areas that are potentially self-damaging, spending, sex, substance abuse, reckless driving, and binge eating. (e) They have recurrent suicidal behavior, gestures, or threats, or self-mutilating behavior. (f) They have affective instability due to marked activity or mood, e.g., intense episodic dysphoria, irritability, or anxiety usually lasting a few hours and only rarely more than a few days. (g) They have chronic feeling of emptiness. (h) These individuals are inappropriate, intense anger, or difficulty controlling anger, e.g., frequent displays of temper, constant anger, and recurrent physical flights. (i) They have transient, stress-related paranoid ideation or severe dissociative symptoms.
>
> (p. 710)

Borderline personality disorder impacts 2% of the population (American Psychiatric Press, 2000, p. 708). Individuals with borderline personality disorder suffer from a negative self-image and intense fears of abandonment. Because of this, these individuals tend to be micromanagers, poor collaborators, and emotionally unstable (Cavaiola & Lavender, 2000).

Narcissistic Personality Disorder

The American Psychiatric Association (2000) defined a narcissistic personality disorder in the DSM-V-TR as the following:

> The essential feature of Narcissistic Personality Disorder is a pervasive pattern of grandiosity (in fantasy and behavior), need for admiration, and lack empathy that begins by early adulthood and is present in a variety of contexts, as indicated by five (or more) of the following: (a) have a grandiose sense of self-importance, exaggerates achievements and talents, or expects to be recognized as superior without commensurate achievements. (b) These individuals are preoccupied with fantasies of unlimited success, power, brilliance, beauty, or ideal love. (c) Narcissistic individuals believe that he or she is "special" and unique and can only be understood by, or should associate with, other special or high-status people or institutions. (d) They require excessive admiration. (e) They have a sense of entitlement, i.e., unreasonable expectations of especially favourable treatment or compliance with his or her expectations. (f) Individuals who suffer from the Narcissistic Personality Disorder are interpersonally exploitive, taking advantage of others to

> achieve his or her own ends. (g) They also lack empathy and are unwilling to recognize or identify with the feelings and needs of others. (h) They are often envious of others or believe that others are envious of him or her. (i) Lastly, narcissistic individuals show arrogant, haughty behaviors or attitudes.
>
> (p. 717)

Individuals that suffer from narcissistic personality disorder make up an estimated 1% of the population. While narcissistic personality disorder is not gender-specific, nearly 75% of those diagnosed with the disorder are male. Leaders that have narcissistic personality disorder believe themselves to be superior to everyone else. Leaders with this disorder will display toxic traits such as entitlement, selfishness, and a severe lack of emotional intelligence (Lubit, 2004, p. 19).

Personality and Leadership

Similar to personality disorders, personality traits also impact leadership behaviors. Studies have reported that personality traits can be a predictor of both positive and negative leadership styles (Ayub et al., 2017; De Hoogh et al., 2015; Grijalva & Newman, 2015; Harms & Spain, 2015; Schyns, 2015). Whether it is knowledge creation capacity (Ayub et al., 2017), agreeableness, and extroversion as indicator for leader success (De Hoogh et al., 2015), or finding similarities between dark characteristics and dimensions of the Big Five model (Guenole, 2014), researchers have noted the benefits of understanding personality traits and their relationship to the leadership phenomenon.

One of the models used within the field of personality theory argues for a five-factor view of personality. This five-factor model (FFM), known as the Big-Five Inventory (BFI), contends that there is a basic structure to personality split up into five parts: Extroversion (the degree to which one is comfortable being assertive, taking control, talkative, outgoing), Agreeableness (generosity, gentleness, kindness, compassion), Conscientiousness (whether one is well-organized and reliable), Neuroticism (degree to which one gets anxious, depressed, or irritable), and Openness to experience (one's ability to self-reflect, innovate, and be creative; De Hoogh et al., 2015; Northouse, 2013).

Judge et al. (2002) did a meta-analysis on 78 leadership and personality studies conducted between 1967 and 1998. Their findings suggested that the factors most strongly associated with leadership in general rated high in extroversion, conscientiousness, openness, and low in neuroticism. According to McGreal (2015), individuals that exhibit toxic traits, such as narcissism, register higher on the Big Five areas of extroversion and neuroticism and lower on the area of agreeableness. McGreal (2015) contends that the higher levels of extroversion allow the individual to cover up the high anxiety and depression that comes from the high neuroticism. These two factors, combined with low agreeableness, can create an individual that can gain power and control quickly and use that power and control to manipulate and coerce others in painful ways.

In a similar study by Bartone et al. (2009), the authors found leaders that scored higher on both extroversion and conscientiousness were considered good leaders by their peers, while those leaders that scored lower on extroversion, conscientiousness, and agreeableness were considered poor leaders by their peers. What is interesting to note is that extroversion has been found to be a predictor of both good and bad leadership (Bartone et al., 2009; De Hoogh et al., 2015; Grijalva & Newman, 2015; Harms & Spain, 2015; McGreal, 2015; Schyns, 2015). Studies suggest that while extroversion can be both good or bad, it is the coupling of extroversion with other Big Five factors that can create a formula for leader toxicity.

References

American Psychiatric Press. (2000). *Diagnostic and statistical manual of mental disorders – DSM-IV-TR*. American Psychiatric Press.

Ayub, N., Alqurashi, S., Al-Yafi, W., & Jehn, K. (2017). Personality traits and conflict management styles in predicting job performance and conflict. *International Journal of Conflict Management, 28*. https://doi.org/10.1108/IJCMA-12-2016-0105

Bartone, P. T., Eid, J., Johnsen, B. H., Laberg, J. C., & Snook, S. A. (2009). Big five personality factors, hardiness, and social judgment as predictors of leader performance. *Leadership & Organization Development Journal, 30*(6), 498–521. http://dx.doi.org/10.1108/01437730910981908

Cavaiola, A. A., & Lavender, N. J. (2000). *Toxic coworkers: How to deal with dysfunctional people on the job*. New Harbinger Publications.

de Haan, E. (2016). The leadership shadow: How to recognize and avoid derailment, hubris and overdrive. *Leadership (London, England), 12*(4), 504–512. https://doi.org/10.1177/1742715015572526

De Hoogh, A. H. B., Den Hartog, D. N., & Nevicka, B. (2015). Gender differences in the perceived effectiveness of narcissistic leaders. *Applied Psychology, 64*(3), 473–498. https://doi.org/10.1111/apps.12015

Fisher, K., Hutchings, K., & Sarros, J. (2010). The "bright" and "shadow" aspects of in extremis leadership. *Military Psychology, 22*(S1), S89–S116. https://doi.org/10.1080/08995601003644346

Goldman, A. (2009). *Transforming toxic leaders*. Stanford University Press. https://doi.org/10.1515/9780804772570

Grijalva, E., & Newman, D. A. (2015). Narcissism and counterproductive work behavior (CWB): Meta-analysis and consideration of collectivist culture, big five personality, and narcissism's facet structure. *Applied Psychology, 64*(1), 93–126. https://doi.org/10.1111/apps.12025

Guenole, N. (2014). Maladaptive personality at work: Exploring the darkness. *Industrial and Organizational Psychology: Perspectives on Science and Practice*, 7, 85–97.

Harms, P. D., & Spain, S. M. (2015). Beyond the bright side: Dark personality at work. *Applied Psychology, 64*(1), 15–24. https://doi.org/10.1111/apps.12042

Hogan, R., & Hogan, J. (2001). Assessing leadership: A view from the dark side. *International Journal of Selection and Assessment*, *9*, 40–51.

Hogan, R., & Kaiser, R. B. (2005). What we know about leadership. *Review of General Psychology*, *9*(2), 169–180. https://doi.org/10.1037/1089-2680.9.2.169

Judge, T., Bono, J., Ilies, R., & Gerhardt, M. (2002). Personality and leadership: A qualitative and quantitative review. *Journal of Applied Psychology*, *87*, 765–780.

Kapuchinski, S. (2007). Recognizing and taming personality disordered individuals in business. *The Journal for Quality and Participation*, *30*(4), 37–40.

Khoo, H., & Burch, G. (2008). The "dark side" of leadership personality and transformational leadership: An exploratory study. *Personality and Individual Differences*, *44*(1), 86–97. https://doi.org/10.1016/j.paid.2007.07.018

Lubit, R. H. (2004). *Coping with toxic managers, subordinates and other difficult people*. Pearson Education Inc.

Mathieu, C., Neumann, C., Hare, R., & Babiak, P. (2014). A dark side of leadership: Corporate psychopathy and its influence on employee well-being and job satisfaction. *Personality and Individual Differences*, *59*, 83–88. https://doi.org/10.1016/j.paid.2013.11.010

McGreal, S. A. (2015). Personality's "big one" and the enigma of narcissism. *Psychology Today*. www.psychologytoday.com/gb/blog/unique-everybody-else/201511/personalitys-big-one-and-the-enigma-narcissism

Nigro, T. (2018). The shadows in healthcare leadership. *Healthcare Management Forum*, *31*(3), 97–102. https://doi.org/10.1177/0840470417745082

Northouse, P. (2013). *Leadership theory and practice* (6th ed.). Sage.

Schyns, B. (2015). Dark personality in the workplace: Introduction to the special issue. *Applied Psychology*, *64*(1), 1–14. https://doi.org/10.1111/apps.12041

5 Followers

Toxic Leader Enablers

Followers are a vital piece of the leadership phenomenon. Without the followers, the leader has no power. Followers can be drawn to leaders who are powerful, confident, and make them feel secure. Many toxic leaders are aware of these needs in their followers and understand how to use their charisma to manipulate their followers into feeling secure (Gallos, 2008; Lipman-Blumen, 2005). Once the followers have this sense of security, the toxic leader can then begin to abuse their power.

According to Kusy and Holloway (2009), there are some types of followers that can enable toxic leaders. These types of followers fall into three categories: toxic protector, toxic buffer, and toxic handler (Kusy & Holloway, 2009). The first, the toxic protector, "safeguards the toxic leader from any danger" (p. 140). The second, the toxic buffer, becomes the mediator between the leader and the rest of the followers. The third, the toxic handler, takes care of any negatives that arise due to the leader's toxic behavior. Where the toxic protectors and toxic buffers are concerned more with protecting the leader, the toxic handler is more focused on protecting the followers from the toxic leader's behavior, as well as fixing any problems that the toxic leader has created. Each one of these types of followers ultimately enables the toxic leader's behavior, which allows them to gain and abuse more power.

Negative Impact on Followers

Gallus et al. (2013) comprehensively described the impact of these toxic leaders on those that follow them:

> Those who experience toxic leadership are more likely to have reduced job satisfaction and organizational commitment and are less likely to engage in organizational citizenship behaviors . . . the impact of toxic leaders does not stop at the individual. Toxic leadership has even been

DOI: 10.4324/9781003202462-5

> found to negatively impact the target's personal relationships in the form of increased partner conflict and higher work–life conflict . . . their behaviors negatively impact [their peers], from higher turnover intentions and drug and alcohol abuse to decreased job satisfaction (i.e., pay, subordinate, co-worker, or supervisor satisfaction), productivity and motivation. Toxic leaders likely understand that the power differential between superiors and subordinates may limit a target's options for responding to the abusive behavior. Indeed, it is likely that most service members feel they cannot push back against their abusive leaders, as doing so would go against the very values they were taught to uphold (e.g., chain of command, mental toughness). Targets who do confront their abusers may be perceived as insubordinate and pursuing options outside one's chain of command would be perceived by most as a violation of cultural norms. When unit members have stronger shared perceptions about the toxic behavior of their leader, we predicted that toxic leadership would have a more substantial negative impact on unit civility. Toxic leadership behavior would have a greater negative effect on job satisfaction and organizational commitment when toxic leadership congruence is high. . . . Targets have been found to have higher stress, greater instances of alcohol abuse, and reduced self-esteem.
>
> (pp. 589–590)

Each of the toxic typologies touched on above can create an unethical, valueless, and selfish leader (de Vries, 2018), which can lead to negative organizational outcomes. These negative organizational outcomes include lower morale, lower levels of productivity, and higher turnover (Cote, 2018; Friedman & Gerstein, 2017; Mohiuddin, 2017). According to Kendrick (2017) and Rousseau and Aubé (2018), there are several long-term negative effects. These are anger and resentment, mistrust, reduced confidence, stalled career development, negative physical health conditions, and negative mental health conditions (Kendrick, 2017, p. 852).

Additionally, research completed by Dobbs and Do (2019) applied a toxic leadership framework from an organizational and leadership perspective to assess the correlation between toxic leadership and organizational cynicism. Dobbs and Do's (2019) conclusions revealed a positive relationship between toxic leadership and organizational contempt. For example, employees who reported having leaders with toxic qualities were likely to have harmful feelings toward their organization, resulting in the follower purposely attempting to sabotage organizational goals, lowering their productivity output, or quitting.

Similarly, Gabriel (2016) conducted a study to empirically examine the association of supervisors' toxicity and subordinates' counterproductive work behavior. Gabriel's study concluded that employees are quick to counter supervisors' toxicity through inefficient work behavior such as shifting anger to either peers or other identifiable assets of the organization.

Parmer and Dillard (2019) also examined the relationship between the perceptions followers have regarding how they are treated in the workplace environment by their current or most recent leader, and how these follower perceptions predicted feelings of power within themselves. What Parmer and Dillard found was that "employees' perceptions and attitudes regarding their immediate supervisor can create positive or negative feelings toward the supervisor which can, in turn, affect the organization's culture and workplace environment, both good and bad" (p. 14).

Further and more recent research conducted by Metin-Orta (2021) added to these findings and outcomes. Metin-Orta's empirical research found that experiences with destructive and toxic leadership had a significant impact on follower's mental and physical well-being. These mental and physical traumas manifested as severe stress, emotional exhaustion, and negative affectivity, all of which has negative impacts on the overall organizational success through decreases in productivity and morale.

These positive and negative feelings touched on by Parmer and Dillard (2019) and Metin-Orta (2021) are expanded on in Webster et al.'s (2016) research. What Webster et al. (2016) discovered were the coping strategies that the followers of toxic leaders used to manage the negative feelings inflicted upon them. Webster et al.'s (2016) research uncovered six behaviors that respondents found toxic. These were manipulating, bullying, emotionally volatile, narcissism, micromanaging, and passive aggressiveness (p. 348). Interaction with these behaviors created psychological, emotional, and physical damage as reported by the study respondents (p. 349). Bond et al. (2016) argued that these toxic behaviors resulted in high increases in post-traumatic stress symptoms.

The psychological, emotional, and physical damage that was sustained led to numerous coping strategies such as:

> instrumental action (e.g. making a formal complaint, seeking mediation and whistle blowing), or information seeking (e.g. seeking professional advice); and emotion-focused strategies such as self-reliance (e.g. working harder), submission (e.g. ruminating), helplessness and delegation (e.g. feelings of shame, self-blame and disgust).
>
> (Webster et al., 2016, pp. 352–353)

Similarly, Li et al.'s (2016) research looked at 248 supervisor–subordinate dyads and found that abusive leaders resulted in followers burning themselves out and overworking as a way to cope with the abusive behavior. Followers in Li et al.'s (2016) study stated that in order to appease their toxic leader, they would simply work harder. Additionally, Harvey et al. (2007) concluded that followers of abusive leaders would experience high levels of emotional exhaustion, resulting in job tensions and turnover intentions. For the followers in Harvey et al.'s (2007) research, the best way to cope with a toxic leader was simply to leave the organization.

Thoroughgood et al. (2012) took a somewhat different approach to the destructive leader–follower dyad. What Thoroughgood et al. (2012) posited was that some followers are drawn to and/or will put up with these destructive leader behaviors for several reasons. These reasons outlined by Thoroughgood et al. (2012) are: (1) follower has negative self-image and seeks approval from the toxic leader, (2) follower is drawn to abusive and authoritative leaders, (3) follower is simply afraid of the leader and therefore complies, (4) followers are toxic themselves and see their toxic leader as a vehicle to acquiring more personal power, and (5) follower holds similar values and goals of the toxic leader, so therefore complies.

Toxic Leader Impact on Organization

Over the years scholars have attempted to assess the financial costs of toxic leadership on an organization. Leyman (1990) calculated that every follower impacted by a toxic leader cost the organization between $30,000 and $100,000 annually (that is between $60,000 and $220,000 in the year 2022) due to the low productivity, turnover, and litigation. Ten years later, Rayner (2000) estimated the replacement costs alone brought on by toxic leaders was $1 million annually. Sheehan (2001) added an estimate of $600,000 to $3.6 million per year for businesses with over 1,000 employees. At a national level, Hoel et al. (2001) estimated the cost of toxic leadership to be $2 billion per year.

Follower Upward Influence

The ability for followers to impact their toxic leader in an attempt to rectify and salvage the negative environments the toxic leaders have helped create is known as ***follower upward influence*** (Epitropaki & Martin, 2013; Carsten & Uhl-Bien, 2012; Kipnis et al., 1980; Liu et al., 2017; Porter et al., 1983; Schriesheim et al., 2000; Yukl et al., 1995). Upward influence has been defined as "attempts to influence someone higher in the formal hierarchy or authority in the organization" (Porter et al., 1983, p. 409) and usually the majority of upward influence attempts are directed at immediate supervisors (e.g., Kipnis et al., 1980). Such attempts are generally aimed at obtaining key benefits from supervisors such as assistance and resources (e.g., Schriesheim et al., 2000; Yukl et al., 1995).

Carsten and Uhl-Bien (2012) contended that upward influence and communication was limited and difficult for followers of toxic leaders. Additionally, Epitropaki and Martin (2013) found that followers of transactional leaders that utilized influence solely through coercion, rewards, and punishments may need to use harder forms of power themselves to influence the toxic leader. Since toxic leaders use coercion to intimidate their followers, followers may need to use the same tactics against them, since this is the only form of influence the toxic leader knows and therefore responds to.

While followers may not have formal authority, it is important for followers to understand what power and influence they hold over their toxic leaders (Kellerman, 2019; Grant et al., 2021). The rise of social media has amplified the influence followers have over the leadership phenomenon. As a new tool of technology, social media allows followers to push and pressure leaders in ways they had not experienced before. Kellerman (2019) argued that followers have an ethical and moral obligation to use this newfound influence and pressure to help change the toxic leader situation in whatever ways are possible.

References

Bond, S. A., Tuckey, M. R., & Dollard, M. F. (2016). Psychosocial safety climate, workplace bullying and symptoms of posttraumatic stress. *Organization Development Journal, 28*(1), 37–56.

Carsten, M. K., & Uhl-Bien, M. (2012). Follower beliefs in the co-production of leadership: Examining upward communication and the moderating role of context. *Journal of Psychology, 220*(4), 210–220. https://doi.org/10.1027/2151-2604/a000115

Cote, R. (2018). Dark side leaders: Are their intentions benign or toxic? *Journal of Leadership, Accountability and Ethics*, 42–65.

De Vries, R. (2018). Three nightmare traits in leaders. *Organizational Psychology, 9*, 871.

Dobbs, J., & Do, J. (2019). The impact of perceived toxic leadership on cynicism in officer candidates. *Armed Forces & Society, 45*(1), 3–26. https://doi.org/10.1177/0095327X17747204

Epitropaki, O., & Martin, R. (2013). Transformational – transactional leadership and upward influence: The role of relative leader – member exchanges (RLMX) and perceived organizational support (POS). *The Leadership Quarterly, 24*(2), 299–315. https://doi.org/10.1016/j.leaqua.2012.11.007

Friedman, H., & Gerstein, M. (2017). Leading with compassion: The key to changing the organizational culture and achieving success (Report). *Psychosociological Issues in Human Resource Management, 5*(1), 160–175. https://doi.org/10.22381/PIHRM5120175

Gabriel, J. (2016). Supervisors' toxicity as predictor of subordinates' counter-productive work behavior in Nigerian public hospitals. *Journal of Applied Business Research, 32*(5), 1363–1374. https://doi.org/10.19030/jabr.v32i5.9765

Gallos, J. V. (2008). Learning from toxic trenches: The winding road to healthier organizations and to healthy everyday leaders. *Journal of Management Inquiry, 17*(234), 354–367.

Gallus, J. A., Walsh, B. M., van Driel, M., Gouge, M. C., & Antolic, E. (2013). Intolerable cruelty: A multilevel examination of the impact of toxic leadership on U.S. military units and service members. *Military Psychology, 25*(6), 588–601. https://doi.org/10.1037/mil0000022

Grant, S., Willsie, S., & Gupta, G. (2021). Thriving in the future: Intentional followership development. *Industrial and Commercial Training, 53*(2), 189–198. https://doi.org/10.1108/ICT-02-2020-0021

Harvey, P., Stoner, J., Hochwarter, W., & Kacmar, C. (2007). Coping with abusive supervision: The neutralizing effects of ingratiation and positive affect on negative employee outcomes. *The Leadership Quarterly, 18*(3), 264–280. https://doi.org/10.1016/j.leaqua.2007.03.008

Hoel, H., Sparks, K., & Cooper, C. (2001). *The cost of violence/stress at work and the benefits of a violence/stress free working environment.* International Labor Organization.

Kellerman, B. (2019). The future of followership. *Strategy & Leadership, 47*(5), 42–46. https://doi.org/10.1108/SL-07-2019-0109

Kendrick, K. (2017). The low morale experience of academic librarians: A phenomenological study. *Journal of Library Administration, 57*(8), 846–878. https://doi.org/10.1080/01930826.2017.1368325

Kipnis, D., Schmidt, S., & Wilkinson, I. (1980). Intraorganizational influence tactics: Explorations in getting one's way. *Journal of Applied Psychology, 65,* 440–452.

Kusy, M., & Holloway, E. (2009). *Toxic workplace: Managing toxic personalities and their systems of power.* John Wiley & Sons Inc.

Leyman, H. (1990). Mobbing and psychological terror at workplaces. *Violence and Victims, 5,* 119–125.

Li, X., Li, X., Qian, J., Qian, J., Han, Z., Han, Z., Jin, Z., & Jin, Z. (2016). Coping with abusive supervision: The neutralizing effects of perceived organizational support and political skill on employees' burnout. *Current Psychology, 35*(1), 77–82. https://doi.org/10.1007/s12144-015-9363-5

Lipman-Blumen, J. (2005). Toxic leadership: When grand illusions masquerade as noble visions. *Leader to Leader, 2005*(36), 29–36. https://doi.org/10.1002/ltl.125

Liu, Song, Z., Li, X., & Liao, Z. (2017). Why and when leaders' affective states influence employee upward voice. *Academy of Management Journal, 60*(1), 238–263. https://doi.org/10.5465/amj.2013.1082

Metin-Orta, I. (2021), The impact of destructive leadership on followers' well-being. In S. M. Camgöz & Ö. T. Ekmekci (Eds.), *Destructive leadership and management hypocrisy* (pp. 101–115). Emerald Publishing Limited. https://doi.org/10.1108/978-1-80043-180-520211007

Mohiuddin, Z. (2017). Influence of leadership style on employees' performance: Evidence from literatures. *Journal of Marketing and Management,* 18–30.

Parmer, L., & Dillard, J. E. (2019). The way employees are treated predict power feelings. *Leadership & Organization Development Journal, 40*(1), 2–16. https://doi.org/10.1108/LODJ-08-2018-0312

Porter, L., Allen, R., & Angle, H. (1983). *The politics of upward influence in organizations Organizational influence processes* (pp. 408–422). Scott, Foresman.

Rayner, C. (2000) Building a business case for tackling bullying in the workplace: beyond a basic cost-benefit approach. In M Sheehan, S Ramsay & J Patrick (eds), *Transcending boundaries: integrating people, processes and systems.* Griffith University, Brisbane, Australia, pp. 31–36.

Rousseau, V., & Aubé, C. (2018). When leaders stifle innovation in work teams: The role of abusive supervision. *Journal of Business Ethics, 151*(3), 651–664. https://doi.org/10.1007/s10551-016-3258-8

Schriesheim, C., Castro, S., & Yammarino, F. (2000). Investigating contingencies: An examination of the impact of span of supervision and upward controllingness on leader – member exchange using traditional and multivariate within and between-entities analysis. *Journal of Applied Psychology, 85,* 659–677.

Sheehan, M., McCarthy, P., Barker, M., & Henderson, M. (2001). A model for assessing the impact and cost of workplace bullying. In *Organizational symbolism.* Trinity College.

Thoroughgood, C., Padilla, A., Hunter, S., & Tate, B. (2012). The susceptible circle: A taxonomy of followers associated with destructive leadership. *The Leadership Quarterly, 23*(5), 897–917. https://doi.org/10.1016/j.leaqua.2012.05.007

Webster, V., Brough. P., & Daly, K. (2016, October). Fight, flight or freeze: Common responses for follower coping with toxic leadership. *Stress Health, 32*(4), 346–354. https://doi.org/10.1002/smi.2626. Epub 2014 Dec 3. PMID: 25470138.

Yukl, G., Guinan, P. & Sottolano, D. (1995). Influence tactics used for different objectives with subordinates, peers, and superiors. *Group and Organization Management, 20*, 272–296.

6 Culture

We broadly discussed the effects of toxic leaders on organizations and followers. We now turn to the relationships between toxic leadership and organizations. Leaders operate within organizational cultures and have a role in setting the organizational culture and climate. Therefore, an organization's culture and climate might create circumstances that enable or dissuade toxic leaders, and toxic leadership may also affect the culture and climate. To understand these effects, we define organizational culture and climate, describe how scholars have viewed the leader's role in setting the culture and climate, then share research on toxic leadership and culture and climate.

Organizational culture and climate are two distinguishing organizational phenomena with distinct theoretical backgrounds (Schein, 1990; Schneider et al., 2017). Organizational culture research has primarily relied on qualitative methods as it emerged from sociology and anthropology traditions. Organizational climate research has been conducted mainly by organizational psychologists from the Gestalt tradition who conceived of climate as the observable summative perceptions of organizational actors based on their shared perceptions of organizational rewards and expectations (Schneider et al., 2017). On the other hand, organizational cultures seem to exist at a more fundamental level of awareness and thus are not always observable. Culture relates to shared values, assumptions, and norms that form a basis for organizational identity, commitment, and action. Organizational cultures are grounded in history, tradition, and collective identity.

According to Schein (1990), psychologists began studying organizational climate in the 1930s but did not systematically study culture until the 1980s. Culture has been difficult to study scientifically (Hofstede, 1980; Schein, 1996) because the concept escaped definition for many years, and it is not always clear what cultural factors might be explained by related phenomena (e.g., climate, leadership, values). Schein (1996) conceived of climate as a surface manifestation of culture, noting that climate is subject to variation (Schein, 1996).

DOI: 10.4324/9781003202462-6

What Is Culture?

Culture refers to "the collective programming of the human mind that distinguishes the members of one human group from those of another" (Hofstede, 1980, p. 24). Early research on culture was associated with differences in national cultures or "that part of our conditioning that we share with other members of our nation, region, or group but not with members of other nations, regions, or groups" (Hofstede, 1983, p. 76). Hofstede (1983) proposed four independent dimensions of national culture: individualism versus collectivism, large or small power distance, strong or weak uncertainty avoidance, and masculinity versus femininity. In 1998, Hofstede and Bond introduced a fifth dimension to national culture, which they described as long-term versus short-term orientation (Minkov & Hofstede, 2011). Hofstede et al. (2010) added a final national culture dimension (indulgence versus restraint).

What Is Organizational Culture?

Hofstede (1980) argued that national cultures shaped what organizational theorists studied, valued, and concluded. Thus, for Hofstede, cultural relativism (the effect of different national cultures) restricted the generalizability of early organizational culture theories. Hofstede et al. (1990) extended the research on national cultures to the organizational context through a series of interviews to examine manifestations of culture as symbols, heroes, rituals, and values. The research was designed to minimize the effects of cultural relativism by crossing national boundaries. The study resulted in a six-factor model for organizational culture: process-oriented versus results-oriented, employee-oriented versus job-oriented, parochial versus professional, open system versus closed system, loose control versus tight control, and normative versus pragmatic. Hofstede et al. (1990) concluded that the dimensions of perceived practices within their six-factor model could be used "as a checklist for practical culture differences between organizations" (p. 305).

One finding was surprising to Hofstede and his colleagues. Determinants of organizational culture were associated with shared perceptions of daily practices, but not values, as hypothesized. Hofstede et al. (1990) concluded that shared values strongly correlated with demographic differences such as nationality, age, and education, but not with membership in an organization. Individuals develop values as they are socialized through their families, religious institutions, schools, and other affiliations. Values are usually set by the age of ten, long before people get to the workforce, so one does not learn their values through organizational indoctrination (Minkov & Hofstede, 2011). This finding has profound implications for organizations. Hiring managers should not look over critical differences in values, hoping that new hires will eventually take on the values of the organization.

Organizational culture affects multiple aspects of an organization (Hofstede, 1980). Culture affects how the dominant coalition distributes power, whose interests are respected, which values take precedence, how decisions are made, the structure and processes, reward systems, worker behavior, and the influence of external stakeholders. The most widely accepted definition of culture is

> (a) a pattern of basic assumptions, (b) invented, discovered, or developed by a given group, (c) as it learns to cope with its problems of external adaptation and internal integration, (d) that has worked well enough to be considered valid and, therefore (e) is to be taught to new members as the (f) correct way to perceive, think, and feel in relation to those problems.
>
> The strength and degree of internal consistency of a culture are, therefore, a function of the stability of the group, the length of time the group has existed, the intensity of the group's experiences of learning, the mechanism by which the learning has taken place (i.e., positive reinforcement or avoidance conditioning), and the strength and clarity of the assumptions held by founders and leaders of the group.
>
> (Schein, 1990, p. 111)

Thus, organizational culture is an enduring aspect of an organization's identity. Organizational members may act in ways that are not in keeping with the culture; however, the culture will pull members back toward the behaviors that are aligned with the accepted norms. Organizational climate, although related, is a more transient phenomenon. There has been a great deal of confusion about the differences between organizational culture and climate. Many scholars agree that climate is a subset of culture and that climate relates to a more temporary construct. In some ways, culture is like personality, while climate is like mood. Personality is an enduring characteristic of individuals. Personality can change over time, but usually in response to systemic changes. Moods, on the other hand, can change rapidly based on temporary circumstances and events, such as weather, food intake, and amount of sleep.

What Is Organizational Climate?

Moran and Volkwein (1992) defined organizational climate as:

> A relatively enduring characteristic of an organization which distinguishes it from other organizations, and (a) embodies members' collective perceptions about their organization with respect to such dimensions as autonomy, trust, cohesiveness, support, recognition, innovation, and fairness; (b) is produced by member interaction; (c) serves as a basis for interpreting the situation; (d) reflect the prevalent norms, values, and

attitudes of the organization's culture; and (e) acts as a source of influence for shaping behavior.

(p. 20)

Researchers have found that organizational climate affects organizational performance and the motivation and behavior of individuals (Moran & Volkwein, 1992). Accordingly, one of the intriguing aspects of organizational climate research is that it has crossed the boundaries between the organizational and individual units of analysis. Glick (1985) argued that organizational climate should be distinguished from psychological climate with the respective units of analysis as the organization versus the individual.

Consequently, organizational climate is developed through shared experiences within an organization in terms of (a) exposure to common structural characteristics, (b) the norming of members through the processes of selection, attraction, and attrition, and (c) the social interactions that lead to shared meaning.

Leadership and Culture

"Leadership and culture are two sides of the same coin" (Schein, 1992, p. 15). Leaders initially create the organizational culture through their actions in creating the organization. Once a culture has evolved, then the culture determines the criteria for leadership. If the culture becomes dysfunctional, then leadership has a responsibility to step back in and fix the culture.

Schein argued that culture acts as a primary source of resistance to "organizational learning, development, and planned change" (Schein, 1992, p. xiv). Culture is difficult to manage in a climate of perpetual change. Consequently, the challenge lies in creating a culture in which learning, innovation, change, and adaptation are the norms.

Culture can be analyzed at three levels: artifacts, espoused values, and basic underlying assumptions (Schein, 1992). Artifacts refer to "phenomena that one sees, hears, and feels when one encounters a new group with an unfamiliar culture" (p. 17). Espoused values are expressed and articulated values that guide a group "as a way of dealing with the uncertainty of intrinsically uncontrollable or difficult events" (p. 20). Members of an organization may act in ways that are incongruent with espoused values, in which case the espoused values are incongruent with the underlying basic assumptions. Basic assumptions are unconscious or subconscious beliefs about how things work that are so ingrained as to be considered true. Changes to basic assumptions require changes to an individual's cognitive structure. The pattern of basic assumptions forms the essence of the culture. In the context of cultural change efforts, it is much easier to diagnose and deal effectively with artifacts and espoused values once one understands the basic assumptions (p. 26).

Leaders reveal basic assumptions through actions and behaviors. Primary embedding mechanisms and secondary articulation and reinforcement mechanisms embed, articulate, and reinforce culture within organizations (Schein, 1992). There are six primary mechanisms and six secondary articulation and reinforcement mechanisms. Primary embedding mechanisms consist of what leaders pay attention to, measure, and control; how leaders respond to incidents and crises; deliberate modeling, mentoring, teaching, and coaching; resource allocation; and criteria for recruitment, selection, promotion, and retirement. Secondary articulation and reinforcement mechanisms are the organizational design and structure; organizational systems and procedures; rites and rituals; physical design of buildings and spaces; stories, legends, and myths; and the organizational philosophy, values, and creed. Secondary mechanisms reinforce the organizational cultures of young organizations. However, these artifacts constrain leaders of mature organizations and become culture-embedding mechanisms (Schein, 1992).

Books on corporate culture often describe a relationship between culture and long-term economic performance, suggesting that stronger cultures, adaptive cultures, and strategically aligned cultures perform better than their opposites (Kotter & Heskett, 1992). Based on a qualitative and quantitative examination of 207 firms from 22 industries, Kotter and Heskett (1992) concluded that adaptive cultures perform better in the long run because leaders effectively transform cultures to respond to changing environmental conditions. Group members of adaptive cultures value leadership, entrepreneurship, and prudent risk-taking. Adaptive cultures are characterized by innovation and flexibility.

Deal and Kennedy (1982) differentiated between strong and weak organizational cultures. Strong organizational cultures provide low ambiguity for group members. Group members adhere to informal rules that evolve as organizational leaders cope with threats to the group's survival. The informal rules dictate how group members act most of the time. Groups with strong cultures have figured out how to succeed within their organizational context. The lessons are inculcated throughout the organization. New members indoctrinate into the culture and adopt the same values and beliefs about what works and how things are accomplished. Strong cultures develop stories about heroes within their organization that exemplify the beliefs and values. Strong cultures share rites and rituals that reinforce desired behaviors and that serve as a visible artifact of what the company's values. Strong cultures have an informal network that serves as the primary way of effectively getting things done and understanding "what's really going on" (Deal & Kennedy, 1982, p. 15).

Weak organizational cultures indicate a troubled business where some employees disagree with established norms, practices, and customs (Ammons, 2021). Weak cultures demonstrate levels of (a) unclear values and beliefs, (b) competing values and beliefs, (c) fundamentally different values and beliefs in different parts of the company, (d) destructive or disruptive heroes, or (e) disorganized or contradictory rituals on how to succeed in their business (Ammons, 2021; Deal & Kennedy, 1982). Symptoms of weak organizational culture are inward or short-term focus; fragmentation and inconsistency; emotional outbursts; ingrown, clashing, or exclusive subcultures; and subcultures that are stronger than the company culture.

What Types of Organizational Cultures Breed Toxic Leaders?

It would be too easy to suggest that any culture that does not promote positive organizational outcomes would lead to negative organizational outcomes. That may be true. Weak cultures demonstrate the absence of effective leadership. We suspect that toxic leaders thrive in organizations that have weak cultures. In those organizations, the culture is not strong enough to push back effectively against the whim of a toxic leader. However, toxic leaders also exist in organizations with strong cultures. So, the truth must be more nuanced.

Our open system model of toxic leadership demonstrated a systems relationship between the organization, the toxic leader, and other organizational stakeholders. Toxic leaders are often politically astute. They fool the people above them through selective sharing of key information, manipulating human resources systems, highlighting underperformance, overstating their own achievements and competence, representing successes as their own, altering behaviors when dealing with superiors, and firing subordinates who get in their way. Some toxic leaders are focused on the growth and performance of business metrics. Those toxic leaders have no regard for their subordinates, except as they contribute to performance metrics. They promote positive results up to their superiors while sucking the life out of subordinates. Furthermore, some toxic leaders have trained followers to cover their tracks, be afraid to push back, stop networking and developing outside relationships, and communicate only through their hierarchy. Finally, followers of toxic leaders also lose interest in their work, disengage from the organization, behave maliciously, suffer health and wellness effects, and underperform their peers.

Based on these aspects of toxic leaders, cultural features may allow toxic leaders to go unnoticed or unchecked. Toxic leaders may flourish in organizational cultures that have (a) a short-term focus, (b) hierarchical command structures, (c) strong silos, (d) protective organizational functions, (e) patriarchal forms, (f) weak cultures, (g) strong subcultures, and (h) weak feedback systems.

Organizations with a short-term focus reward short-term performance (especially financial measures), seek immediate gratification, tolerate moral hazard, and punish mistakes (Brochet et al., 2015). Such organizations tend to starve employee development, ignore danger signals related to long-term concerns, and silence perspectives that bring attention to systemic problems. Organizations with a short-term focus have inconsistent quality and unacceptable error rates (HR Focus, 2004), ultimately choking innovation because managers are more concerned with immediate outputs (Cote, 2008). Toxic leadership flourishes as leaders have a green light to use employees for short-term gains and not worry about the fallout. Employees who burn out will quit or be fired, thus creating a replacement cycle with fresh employees. Systems in these organizations will often thrive off competition instead of cooperation, further reducing the likelihood that leaders will act against toxic leaders below them.

Hierarchical, command-and-control organizations emphasize strong adherence to chain of command. These organizations discourage employees from making strong vertical connections with upper- or lower-level employees who do not connect directly through the organizational chart. Thus, employees are dependent on direct supervisors for communication, performance evaluation, compensation, training, development, promotion, resources, and transmission of organizational values. Toxic leaders put their oppressed followers on an island, effectively marooned from sources of relief or comfort. Toxic leaders poison other organizational actors to believe that the oppressed followers are bad actors, thus further alienating the individuals.

Siloed organizations emphasize unit or departmental identity to the exclusion of other units and departments. Therefore, these organizations discourage networking across boundaries. Employees cannot formulate connections or observe healthy behaviors in other parts of the organization. Silos operate similarly to hierarchy, preventing the exchange of ideas, information, and resources that employees need to protect themselves from toxic leaders.

Organizations with strong protective functions rally resources around protecting the mothership. The human resource, legal, compliance, risk management, and other functions will vigorously battle any threat to the organization, even when the perceived threat is an employee making a valid complaint against a manager. The protective instinct is particularly pronounced when the organizational or subunit identity is so strong that people willfully look the other way to protect the organization's reputation.

Patriarchal organizations are determined by familial, gender-, or race-based relationships. These organizations often demonstrate in-group favoritism and allow individuals within the in-group to thrive while limiting opportunities for individuals in the out-group. In-group favoritism is deferential or discriminatory intergroup tendencies related to behaviors, attitudes, preferences, and perceptions (Turner et al., 1979). In-group members hold the alliances, manage the resources, and control performance evaluations. Out-group members lack agency and the ability to control their situations. Deferential or discriminatory treatment does not need to be overt or explicit. In-group members hold implicit biases that operate beneath the surface of their consciousness, resulting in systemic favoritism that disadvantages the out-group members.

Weaker cultures are characterized by unclear or competing values, beliefs, and rituals and destructive or disruptive heroes (Deal & Kennedy, 1982). Toxic leaders can take advantage of widespread disagreement on norms, a lack of commitment to shared values and practices, and misalignment in goals and objectives (Ammons, 2021). Likewise, strong subcultures operate at cross purposes from the overall organizational culture. A strong subculture offers a competing, sometimes destructive, culture, thus weakening the central culture. Johnson (2021) suggested that subcultures often spoil organizational compliance and drive cynicism, burnout, and emotional strife.

Organizations with weak feedback systems keep problems from surfacing. Toxic leaders present their stories upward to their managers and outward to support functions (e.g., human resources and legal departments). Toxic leaders undermine their employees by taking credit for successes, exploiting gaps and weaknesses, and cutting employees from access to support systems. Employees effectively are silenced because the organization is aware of the issues.

How Do Toxic Leaders Affect Organizational Climate?

According to Jones and James (1979), there are six dimensions of organizational climate:

1. Leadership facilitation and support
2. Workgroup cooperation, friendliness, and warmth
3. Professional and organizational esprit
4. Job challenge, importance, and variety
5. Mutual trust

Organizational climate is associated with leadership outcomes (Bamel et al., 2013; Fitzgibbons, 2018). A critical difference between culture and climate is that leaders can determine climate, whereas some aspects of culture rely on forces external to the leaders. (Wallace et al., 1999). Toxic leadership outcomes affect employees' collective attitudes, behaviors, and feelings toward the organization (Brochet et al., 2012; Schein, 2009; Schneider et al., 2017). The effects of toxic leadership can extend beyond individuals and workgroups. Feelings of apathy, fear, frustration, hopelessness, humiliation, inadequacy, miserableness, resentment, and stress lead to collective avoidance behaviors, emotional contagion, ganging up, internal struggle, and selective accountability. Toxic leaders slowly poison the organizational climate until they destroy the culture. Toxic leadership outcomes include attrition, division of followers, inefficiency, lack of respect, lack of unit discipline, errors, snowball effects, and the firing of the toxic leader or followers.

Leaders embed, articulate, and reinforce culture within organizations through primary and secondary articulation and reinforcement mechanisms.

When organizational leaders create situations that enable or effectively ignore toxic leaders, they signal that such toxic behaviors are acceptable or not significant enough to warrant their attention. The primary cultural embedding mechanisms will signal that toxic behaviors are welcomed within the culture. Secondary articulation and reinforcement mechanisms will eventually change as the culture weakens or changes. We predict that the culture would shift toward a short-term focus, hierarchy, silos, over-protection, weak culture, strong subcultures, and weakened feedback systems.

References

Ammons, D. L. (2021). *Leading or misleading: The impact of leadership change on organizational culture* [Doctoral dissertation, University of Maryland]. ProQuest Dissertations Publishing.

Bamel, U. K., Rangnekar, S., Stokes, P., & Rastogi, R. (2013). Organizational climate and managerial effectiveness: An Indian perspective. *International Journal of Organizational Analysis, 21*(2), 198–218. https://doi.org/10.1108/IJOA-09-2011-0514

Brochet, F., Loumioti, M., & Serafeim, G. (2015). Speaking of the short-term: Disclosure horizon and managerial myopia. *Review of Accounting Studies, 20*(3), 1122–1163. https://doi.org/10.1007/s11142-015-9329-8

Brochet, F., Serafeim, G., & Loumioti, M. (2012). Short-termism: Don't blame investors. *Harvard Business Review, 90*(6), 28. https://go.exlibris.link/tXB2mhWN

Cote, M. (2008). *There are shareholders, and then* (Vol. 141, p. 68). https://go.exlibris.link/8p54Svp7

Deal, T. E., & Kennedy, A. A. (1982). *Corporate cultures: The rites and rituals of corporate life*. Addison-Wesley.

Fitzgibbons, K. A. (2018). *The relation between toxic leadership and organizational climate: An investigation into the existence of toxic leadership within an organization and the effects those toxic elements have on organizational climate* (Publication Number Dissertation/Thesis) ProQuest Dissertations Publishing. https://go.exlibris.link/mW6NxcWy

Glick, W. H. (1985). Conceptualizing and measuring organizational and psychological climate: Pitfalls in multilevel research. *The Academy of Management Review, 10*(3), 601–616. https://doi.org/10.2307/258140

Hofstede, G. (1980). Culture and organizations. *International Studies of Management & Organization, 10*(4), 15–41. https://doi.org/10.1080/00208825.1980.11656300

Hofstede, G. (1983). The cultural relativity of organizational practices and theories. *Journal of International Business Studies, 14*(2), 75–89. https://doi.org/10.1057/palgrave.jibs.8490867

Hofstede, G., Hofstede, G. J., & Minkov, M. (2010). *Cultures and organizations: Software of the mind: Intercultural cooperation and its importance for survival* (3rd ed.). McGraw-Hill.

Hofstede, G., Neuijen, B., Daval Ohayv, D., & Sanders, G. (1990). Measuring organizational cultures: A qualitative and quantitative study across twenty cases. *Administrative Science Quarterly, 35*(2), 286–316. https://doi.org/10.2307/2393392

HR Focus. (2004). Multiple employer initiatives: Working for better health care. *HR Focus: Generic, 81*, 11. https://go.exlibris.link/jrSCWkxX

Johnson, S. M. (2021). *An exploration of the impact of organizational subculture on ethical decision making in policing* [Doctoral dissertation, Walden University]. ProQuest Dissertations Publishing.

Jones, A. P., & James, L. R. (1979). Psychological climate: Dimensions and relationships of individual and aggregated work environment perceptions [article]. *Organizational Behavior and Human Performance*, *23*(2), 201–250. https://doi.org/10.1016/0030-5073(79)90056-4

Kotter, J. P., & Heskett, J. L. (1992). *Corporate culture and performance*. Free Press, Maxwell Macmillan International.

Minkov, M., & Hofstede, G. (2011). The evolution of Hofstede's doctrine. *Cross Cultural Management*, *18*(1), 10–20. https://doi.org/10.1108/13527601111104269

Moran, E. T., & Volkwein, J. F. (1992). The cultural approach to the formation of organizational climate. *Human Relations*, *45*(1).

Schein, E. H. (1990). Organizational culture. *The American Psychologist*, *45*(2), 109–119. https://doi.org/10.1037/0003-066X.45.2.109

Schein, E. H. (1992). *Organizational culture and leadership* (2nd ed.). Jossey-Bass.

Schein, E. H. (1996). Culture: The missing concept in organization studies. *Administrative Science Quarterly*, *41*(2), 229–240. https://doi.org/10.2307/2393715

Schein, E. H. (2009). *The corporate culture survival guide* (2nd ed., Vol. 158). Jossey-Bass. https://go.exlibris.link/y8kD6HzY

Schneider, B., González-Romá, V., Ostroff, C., & West, M. A. (2017). Organizational climate and culture: Reflections on the history of the constructs in the journal of applied psychology. *Journal of Applied Psychology*, *102*(3), 468–482. https://doi.org/10.1037/apl0000090

Turner, J. C., Brown, R. J., & Tajfel, H. (1979). Social comparison and group interest ingroup favouritism [article]. *European Journal of Social Psychology*, *9*(2), 187–204. https://doi.org/10.1002/ejsp.2420090207

Wallace, J., Hunt, J., & Richards, C. (1999). The relationship between organisational culture, organisational climate and managerial values. *The International Journal of Public Sector Management*, *12*(7), 548–564. https://doi.org/10.1108/09513559910305339

7 Model

Toxic leaders are regularly portrayed and sometimes glorified on the big screen. David Nusair (2019) published a list of the "Top 10 Bad Bosses" in movies. The list included Buddy Ackerman in *Swimming with Sharks*; Darth Vader from *Star Wars*; John Milton from *Devil's Advocate*; Bernie Lomax of *Weekend at Bernie's*; Miranda Priestly from *The Devil Wears Prada*; Blake from *Glengarry Glen Ross*; Dick Jones from *RoboCop*; Bill Lumbergh from *Office Space*; Avery Tolar from *The Firm*; and Franklin Hart Jr. from *9 to 5*. Baroness von Hellman from *Cruella* plays a toxic leader and mother! Also, consider military examples such as Jack Nicholson's character, Colonel Nathan R. Jessep, in *A Few Good Men* and the unforgettable Gunnery Sergeant Hartman in *Full Metal Jacket*, played by R. Lee Ermey.

The sad reality is that art imitates life. The stories we've heard are as devastating as those depicted in the movies, except the stakes were real. Toxic leaders do actual harm to their followers. Reputations are tarnished, careers are derailed, and lives are upended. Consider recent news accounts of toxic leadership.

USA Today's Hannah Yasharoff reported (Yasharoff, 2021): Two top CBS execs on leave after *LA Times* investigation alleged racist, misogynistic culture, reports say:

> *Two of CBS's top executives are on administrative leave following a Los Angeles Times investigation that alleged the cultivating of a toxic workplace, including a culture of racism and misogyny, according to reports.*
>
> "Peter Dunn, President of the CBS Television Stations, and David Friend, Senior Vice President, News for the TV Stations, have been placed on administrative leave, pending the results of a third-party investigation into issues that include those raised in a recent *Los Angeles Times* report," *read a CBS statement obtained by CNN Business and The Hill.*
>
> *Friend had a track record of using insults and expletives with employees, allegations in the* Times *report claimed. He said in a statement to the news outlet that he has a "strong track record of hiring, supporting and placing women and BIPOC journalists in important roles as anchors, reporters and news directors," and that his comments were made on the basis of performance, not race or gender.*

DOI: 10.4324/9781003202462-7

NPR's Daniel Zwerdling reported (Zwerdling, 2014) "Army Takes on Its Own Toxic Leaders":

> *Costabile says he never heard the term toxic leadership while he was in the Army. But he says some of his own leaders started tormenting him psychologically three years ago in Afghanistan, and the abuse continued when he came home in 2011 to Fort Carson in Colorado. He says those leaders didn't scream at him, they ostracized him. And the more he felt like he was falling apart, the worse it got. Army records show he had "major depressive episodes" and "multiple hospitalizations."*
>
> *"Like the kid that was picked last for kickball in school, you know? I get the jobs that nobody wanted to do. Take out the trash, you're going to sweep the floor, you're going to mop the hallway. And it's like, why?" Costabile says.*
>
> *Army records show that Costabile stopped eating more than a few bites each day; he lost 30 pounds in a month. His wife found him lying on the bathroom floor after he took dozens of antidepressants and other pills. But some officers said he was faking it.*
>
> *"And I just had feelings, like, that nothing's ever going to change," Costabile says. "I'm going to get [expletive] every day, and I just don't want this anymore. And I just felt like I wanted to kill myself."*

Stephanie Hinshaw (Hinshaw, 2019) blogged:

> *I graduated from college and started my career. I was fortunate to work for individuals who cared about me and my development. Because of their mentoring and my natural ability and grit, I started to rise in my career. I continued this way for many years – excelling, feeling supported, and learning. I furthered my education and earned an MBA and my success in my career continued to rise.*
>
> *And then everything changed. Specifically, I had a change in the individual(s) I reported to at work. Instead of feeling successful, I started feeling like a failure. Instead of having a work–life balance, all I did was work and worry about work. I received inappropriate messages and phone calls at all hours of the day (or night). I watched people being ridiculed, fired, and belittled on a daily basis (And on many occasions, I was that person being ridiculed or belittled.) When I did not want to engage in those behaviors, I was "coached" to act differently.*
>
> *I started not being able to sleep at night, making bad decisions, not liking myself, and having great feelings of anxiety. And through all of this, I always thought the problem was me. I thought I was causing this, that I needed to change, that I was not good enough.*

These are sensational stories, but they are not unusual. It seems that everyone has experienced a toxic leader. Walker began collecting stories about toxic leaders in a course he taught on toxic leadership. Eventually, he had gathered over 300 stories, of which 130 were suitable for analysis. The remainder of the chapter will describe the results of two studies that the authors undertook based on Walker's collection of toxic stories.

Our Research

Word Frequency Analysis

We began by conducting a word frequency analysis using the "grouping by stem words" feature of NVivo 12. Grouping by stem words is a feature that aggregates words with the same base (e.g., behave, behaving, behavior, and behaviors code under the base word behavior). We removed stop words that would not be helpful to the analysis (e.g., toxic, leader, leadership, follower, experience) and short words (i.e., words with fewer than five characters) from the query. Based on the setup described, the ten most-frequent words were behavior, environment, dysfunctional, morale, created, destructive, negative, style, cause, and qualities.

We examined the sentences that contained each of the top ten words generated through the word frequency analysis. Representative words found near "behavior" coded around dysfunctional, aggressive, destructive, selfish, toxic, unethical, and threatening. "Environment" coded around toxic, stressful, negative, depressing, and uncomfortable. "Dysfunctional" coded near leaders, leadership, behaviors, personal characteristics, organizations, and actions. "Morale" was associated with a reduction or destruction of morale. "Creating" was often associated with a toxic work environment or other adverse outcomes. "Destructive" was associated with leaders, leadership, and behavior or the concept of being destructive to followers. "Negative" was associated with emotions, expectations, climate, outcomes, impact, attitudes, qualities, and leadership. "Style" was associated with autocratic, top-down, toxic, bad, poor, rigid, stern, Machiavellian, and neurotic. The word "cause" was typically associated with the concept that a leader had caused negative results such as turnover, damage, harm, delays, or a hostile environment. "Qualities" was most often associated with toxic leadership qualities.

Figure 7.1 depicts the 100 most-frequent stemmed words, excluding the stop words. The relative font size within the word cloud is representative of the frequency of the stemmed words. For example, the word behavior was coded 98 times within the 175 cases, dysfunctional was coded 42 times, and intimidate was coded 9 times.

Thematic Analysis

We then performed thematic analysis on the 130 follower experiences using NVivo 12 software.

Figure 7.1 Word cloud of the 100 most-frequent word stems

Automatically Coded Themes and Subthemes

NVivo's automatic coding routine yielded 11 themes: behavior, employees, environment, leaders, leadership, manager, personal, toxic, toxic leader, toxic leadership, and work. Table 7.1 provides the number of subthemes, cases, and references for each theme.

Each of the automatically coded themes contained numerous subthemes. For example, 47 automatically coded subthemes came from the behavior theme and 120 subthemes from the leadership theme. The Cases column refers to the number of cases where NVivo automatically coded each theme. The References column refers to the number of times the themes coded automatically within the total number of cases.

The automatic coding produced several useful subthemes. Many "behavior" subthemes related to types of toxic behaviors that participants reported. Some of the "employee" subthemes related to participants' responses. The "environment" subthemes described the types of toxic environments encountered. The "leaders," "leadership," "management," "toxic," "toxic leader," and "toxic leadership" themes contained subthemes that described toxic leader styles, characteristics, traits, and behaviors. The "personal" theme related to toxic personality descriptors. Finally, the "work" theme contained subthemes related to toxic characteristics of the workplace.

Table 7.1 reports themes generated through automatic coding.

Manually Coded Themes and Subthemes

We completed an initial review of the documents to develop a general understanding of the data. Three broad categories emerged related to (a) toxic leader behaviors, (b) toxic organizational climates, and (c) the outcomes of toxic situations. Within these categories, we coded and organized nodes into themes and subthemes.

The first category, toxic leader behaviors, were actions that participants perceived to be toxic or that created a toxic environment. Toxic leader behaviors included the themes of aberrant behaviors, abuse of power, egocentrism, emotional dysregulation, ineffective leader behaviors, and moral corruption. We divided the six themes of toxic leader behaviors into subthemes. The "aberrant" theme included subthemes of narcissism and paranoia. The "abuse of power" theme included abuse of positional authority and degrading. The "egocentrism" theme included claiming others' ideas, favoritism, greed, hypocrisy, selfishness, suspicion, and transference. The "emotional dysregulation" theme included subthemes of lacking emotional intelligence, lacking emotional regulation, lacking empathy, and lashing out and punishing. The "ineffective leader behaviors" theme included blaming, ignoring feedback, infighting, jumping to conclusions, lacking military bearing, micromanaging, overreacting,

Table 7.1 NVivo Automatically Coded Themes

Theme	*Subthemes*	*Cases*	*References*
Behavior	47	53	91
Employees	67	40	77
Environment	42	56	86
Leaders	120	99	281
Leadership	126	107	308
Manager	73	52	108
Personal	59	54	102
Toxic	62	101	264
Toxic leader	7	54	82
Toxic leadership	12	56	89
Work	68	67	117

setting unclear expectations, and setting unrealistic targets. Finally, the "moral corruption" theme contained subthemes of discrimination, instilling fear, systemic oppression, threatening, and unethical behavior. Some remarks coded under multiple subthemes. For example, the following passage was coded under the subthemes "ignoring feedback" and "claiming others' ideas":

> *I had a manager who only cared about his own opinion and did not listen to feedback. The organization I worked in valued all employee feedback, and most would provide ways to improve workplace procedure and involvement. We took this feedback to our manager, but he completely disregarded it. If he did take the feedback, he claimed it as his own.*

The second category, toxic organizational climates, consisted of the organizational climate themes of attitudes, collective behaviors, and feelings that participants described. The "attitude" theme included subthemes of low morale, low motivation, and low trust. The "collective behaviors" theme included subthemes of avoidance, emotional contagion, ganging up, internal struggle, and selective accountability. The "feelings" theme included subthemes of apathy, fear, frustration, hopelessness, humiliation, inadequacy, miserableness, resentment, and stress.

Participants shared four different reactions to toxic situations. They sometimes deployed coping mechanisms such as strengthening their bonds with other oppressed followers, surviving the situation through increased dedication to the mission, or they took the situation in their stride. They also described situations in which the toxic leaders created environments that recruited other leaders and followers, resulting in a snowball effect where others began to participate in the toxic behavior. Some participants described confronting or talking to toxic leaders to attempt to resolve the situations. Finally, some participants described stepping up and confronting toxic leaders head-on.

The last category, outcomes, contained the themes of organizational outcomes and personal outcomes. The "organizational outcomes" theme consisted of the subthemes of attrition, division of followers, inefficiency, lack of respect, lack of unit discipline, making mistakes, snowball effect, strengthened bonds, and the toxic leader being fired. The "personal outcomes" themes contained subthemes of the follower spoke to the toxic leader, stepping up, surviving through dedication, taking it in stride, and reflecting. Participants sometimes wrote about how toxic situations had been resolved.

Table 7.2 shows the manual themes and subthemes related to toxic leader behaviors, Table 7.3 relates to the organizational outcomes, Table 7.4 reports the themes related to organizational climate, and Table 7.4 describes the follower coping strategies.

Table 7.2 Manually Coded Themes around Toxic Behavior

Theme	*Subthemes*
Aberrant	Narcissism
	Paranoia
Abuse of power	Abuse of positional authority
	Degrading
Egocentrism	Claiming other's ideas
	Favoritism
	Greed
	Hypocrisy
	Selfishness
	Suspicion
	Transference
Emotional dysregulation	Lacking emotional intelligence
	Lacking emotional regulation
	Lacking empathy
	Lashing out
	Punishing
Ineffective leader behaviors	Blaming
	Ignoring feedback
	Infighting
	Jumping to conclusions
	Lacking military bearing
	Micromanaging
	Overreacting
	Setting unclear expectations
	Setting unrealistic targets
Moral corruption	Discrimination
	Instilling fear
	Systemic oppression
	Threatening
	Unethical

Table 7.3 Manually Coded Themes of Organizational Outcomes

Theme	*Subthemes*
Organizational outcomes	Attrition
	Inefficiency
	Division of followers
	Snowball effect
	Toxic leader fired
	Strengthened follower bonds
	Making mistakes
	Lack of unit discipline
	Lack of respect

Table 7.4 Manually Coded Themes Around Organizational Climate

Theme	*Subthemes*
Feelings	Apathy Fear Inadequacy Stress Frustration Hopelessness Humiliation Miserableness Resentment
Collective behaviors	Selective accountability Emotional contagion Avoidance Internal struggle Ganging up
Attitudes	Low morale Low trust Low motivation

Table 7.5 Manually Coded Themes of Follower Coping Strategies

Theme	*Subthemes*
Coping strategy	Spoke to the toxic leader Stepped up performance levels Did not recognize the toxic situation until later reflection Took the situation in stride Survived because of commitment to the organization

Discussion

The study supported the extant literature that toxic leader behaviors harm the psychological and emotional health of their followers (Anjum et al., 2018; Han et al., 2017; Wegge et al., 2014). The study also provided evidence supporting the toxic leadership literature that toxic leadership poisons organizational climates and devalues organizational outcomes (Dobbs & Do, 2019; Gabriel, 2016; Kendrick, 2017).

Toxic Leader Behaviors

The automatic and manual coding exercises revealed numerous leader behaviors that participants perceived as toxic. The automatic coding revealed 47 toxic leader subthemes, of which 24 subthemes contained negative sentiment. As previously discussed, we manually grouped toxic leader behaviors into six themes, which we further divided into 29 subthemes. We compared the automatically generated and manually generated themes and found that the manual themes provided superior insight and context over the manually generated themes.

Some toxic leaders demonstrated behaviors that participants suggested could be classified as clinical disorders and, in some cases, as morally corrupt. These toxic leaders would undoubtedly fall under the label of seriously toxic leaders, as described by Ong et al. (2016). Some participants reported that toxic leaders abused their power and authority and degraded their followers. Many participants described egocentric behavior that suggested toxic leaders who were more concerned with their own needs than the needs of their followers or their organizations. The previous two themes demonstrate the negative traits of dishonesty, disagreeableness, and carelessness reported by Kets de Vries and Miller (1985). Some participants also described toxic leaders who could not regulate their emotions and who lacked empathy for their followers. Other behaviors were more typical of new or inexperienced leaders. One possible explanation for this behavior lies in the way that military organizations place new officers with experienced enlisted personnel. Senior enlisted personnel might notice and report ineffective leader behaviors.

The gamut of negative behaviors ranged from self-serving and petty to demeaning and unlawful. One participant wrote about a supervisor who

> *would degrade me in front of others for simple mistakes (which others made all the time). He would deny requests that I would make, while approving the same requests made by [a colleague]. Someone who was supposed to be my leader, the one I look up to, unjustly discriminated against me.*

Another participant wrote about a particularly dark environment:

> *The lack of discipline, subordinates' fear, and respect for the uniform destroyed my unit from the inside out. People felt they would not be held accountable for their actions, so they raped, did drugs, were drunk and disorderly, and failed to maintain their warfighting standards.*

Some situations left a significant emotional mark on the participants and contributed to harmful outcomes for the organizations.

> *Due to the excessive self-rewarded bonuses, we were running out of money in the department and soon had to downsize. This is where things really started to hit the fan. Management was on the verge of being investigated. In the meantime, employee layoffs were like a game of musical chairs. If you came into the office and had a box on your desk, it was your turn to go. Everyone who backed management up basically had immunity from layoff until the very end.*

The participant indicated that the management team was corrupt and playing favorites. The unethical behavior contributed to a toxic environment in which management fired employees who followed the rules while rewarding those who played along with the unethical behavior with bonuses and job security. Thus the situation created personal distress and, ultimately, organizational failure, consistent with themes outlined in the literature (Cote, 2018; Friedman & Gerstein, 2017; Mohiuddin, 2017).

Organizational Climate and Outcomes

As previously discussed, toxic leadership is a lead predictor of organizational dysfunction (Matos et al., 2018; Mohiuddin, 2017). Organizational climate consists of collective attitudes, behaviors, and feelings toward the organization. The participants in the current study described attitudes of low morale, motivation, and trust. Participants and their colleagues experienced feelings of apathy, fear, frustration, hopelessness, humiliation, inadequacy, miserableness, resentment, and stress. Some participants described collective behaviors of avoidance, emotional contagion, ganging up, internal struggle, and selective accountability. A toxic leader poisons the organizational climate and, if left unchecked, will eventually destroy the culture.

The participants observed destructive organizational outcomes such as attrition, division of followers, inefficiency, lack of respect, lack of unit discipline, errors, snowball effects, and the firing of the toxic leader. In response to these outcomes, some participants reported that they attempted to speak to the toxic leader in an attempt to resolve the situation. Some reported stepping up and providing alternative leadership to the toxic leader. For example,

> *I did not end up getting any recognition; however, the way in which I lead (in the very limited way I could) changed. I started to actively lead from the front. I took initiative, questioned bad orders, and paved a road that ultimately led the way to the leader I have become today.*

Some participants described how they survived the situation by dedicating themselves to the organization and putting up with the behavior or taking the toxic leadership in stride. Finally, some participants described how they did not realize until further reflection that they were involved in a toxic situation until after they left the organization.

Toxic Leader Archetypes

The study revealed six toxic leader archetypes. There is some overlap in behaviors between the archetypes. For example, toxic leaders of any type might promote misinformation to their managers to make themselves look good and their followers look bad.

Aberrant Behavior

According to Ong et al. (2016), leaders that could be categorized as having irregular or eccentric behavior can carry many attractive leadership qualities and traits. Ong et al. (2016) suggest that these emergent leadership behaviors that are common in aberrant leaders are what get these individuals into their leadership positions in the first place. Leaders that carry these aberrant behaviors can appear outgoing, hardworking, and charismatic. However, over time, these qualities and traits that were seen as positive at the start can begin to decrease as the individual spends more time around the followers they are assigned to. Once the followers become more acquainted with the leader and their deviant and toxic style begins to emerge, followers become more disengaged, and their productivity drops significantly.

Similarly, Raskin and Terry (1988) found that aberrant individuals can convey positive leadership traits such as confidence and extraversion. However, these positive leadership traits do not translate into positive leader performance over the long term (Rosenthal & Pittinsky, 2006). This is due to the fact that while these leaders have high confidence levels and are primarily extroverted, which are two indicators of successful leadership, they also include the negative traits such as high lust for power, manipulation, sensitivity to criticism, poor listening and communication skills, and lack of empathy (Kets de Vries & Miller, 1985; Maccoby, 2000).

Abuse of Power

For Baloyi (2020), toxic leadership consists of the inappropriate use of personal power. These leaders usually use hard forms of power that are coercive and manipulative in nature, resulting in the abuse and degradation of employees. This includes leaders who abuse their positions of authority by consistently degrading their employees, ridiculing their employees in public, coercing employees to undergo physical and psychological pains, and promoting divisiveness between colleagues (Baloyi, 2020). By doing this, these leaders create environments of poor morale, stress, anxiety, depression, distrust, fear, high turnover, everyone for themselves culture, low growth, low motivation, and an increase in litigation on their firms. Kendrick (2017) affirmed these findings in her research on power abusing leaders, arguing that employees who "experience low morale exhibit numerous negative emotional, physical, and cognitive symptoms; they begin to disengage from their work; and they actively distance themselves from the [organization's] social and professional spheres" (p. 876).

Egocentrism

Wegge et al. (2014), Rasool et al. (2018), and Han et al. (2017) concluded in their research that egocentric leadership styles impact overall employee health, wellness, creativity, and productivity. Matos et al. (2018) also found that an egocentric leader showing behaviors of greed, selfishness, and hypocrisy resulted in negative views of the organization and negative feelings of well-being and self-worth. Their findings suggested that the influence of an egocentric style of leadership, and the corrupt environment that this kind of leadership creates, has damaging effects on the employee's performance and creativity (Han et al., 2017; Rasool et al., 2018; Wegge et al., 2014). Psychologists have also found that negative emotions are especially contagious and have an overwhelmingly adverse effect on the moods of followers (Daft, 2014). When leaders act and behave selfishly, the followers respond by being selfish and egocentric themselves.

Emotional Dysregulation

According to Gabriel (2016), a severe lack of emotional intelligence is what defines a toxic leader. Emotional dysregulation in leadership results in workplace environments riddled with fear and high turnover. Friedman and Gerstein (2017) echoed this conclusion, stating that the Millennial age demographic is especially allergic to emotionless leadership. Similarly, Maamari and Majdalani (2017) contended organizations that "attempt to build on the improvement of the EI of their employees and leaders will first decrease their organizational turnover and decrease the costs of recruitment, training, and adaptation of the new human assets" (p. 345).

Ineffective

In a study conducted by Paltu and Brouwers (2020), leadership that consisted of behaviors such as micromanaging, blaming, and setting unrealistic goals led to organizational toxicity. These toxic behaviors resulted in toxic organizational cultures where employees were less committed to the organization, which led to higher turnover rates and low levels of job satisfaction and productivity (p. 6). Dobbs (2014), Burns (2021), and Schmidt (2014) found in a similar study that leaders that are seen as ineffective, blaming others, unpredictable, and unreliable also have deleterious effects on the overall organization and its outcomes. Dobbs (2014), Burns (2021), and Schmidt's (2014) findings were nearly identical to the findings of Paltu and Brouwers (2020) in that these toxic traits of a leader led to toxic organizational cultures with high turnover, low morale, and low creativity.

Moral Corruption

Cote (2018) contended that the darker styles of leadership were the result of moral-less and unethical leadership. For Cote, unethical leader behaviors would include lying, bullying, use of fear and coercion to influence followers, and corruption. These behaviors displayed by leadership result in organizational climates that hinder creativity and productivity and lowers morale. Similarly, Rasool et al. (2018), Burns (2021), and Han et al. (2017) showed in their research that unethical leader behavior had detrimental effects on organizational environments and cultures. Morally corrupt leaders create toxic climates that lead to mental health issues among employees. Employees who reported experiencing unethical leaders reported creativity drain, sleep deprivation, and emotional exhaustion.

Toxic Leadership Model

As we uncovered themes and subthemes, a model of toxic leadership emerged. It became evident that some participants labeled a leader's actions as toxic, whereas other followers involved in that situation might not have considered the actions to be toxic. Thus, the toxic environment develops from the interaction of the leader with a follower or group of followers and the perceptions of those followers about the intentions and reasons for the leader's actions.

Consider a performance improvement conversation between a manager and a subordinate. The subordinate's view of that conversation might depend on a host of factors, some of which are outside of the manager's control or knowledge. Both the manager and the subordinate react to the situation and to each other in real time. Each picks up cues such as body language, tone, and inflection from the other. Each has private intentions and circumstances that might affect the conversation (e.g., one has not eaten all day), and each has a view of whatever led up to the conversation. It is easy to see how either might view something as negative that was not intended as it came across. These situations can then turn into a downward spiral of negative emotions that result in a toxic label. Over time, the employee could conclude that he or she is operating in a toxic environment. On the other hand, if the employee believed that the leader was making a reasonable and bona fide attempt to help, he or she would not likely label the environment. Thus, whether an employee views an environment as toxic is heavily influenced by how the employee perceives the leader's intentions, whether positive or negative.

The closed system model of toxic leadership (Figure 7.2) models the relationship between the toxic leader and the oppressed follower. Toxic leaders and their oppressed followers eventually engage in a vicious cycle in which each negative experience adds to the overall toxicity. The negative shared experiences reinforce negative mental models, further confirmed by negative spins on situational outcomes. Shared experiences take on a negative connotation within their mental models such that they cannot process new situations outside of a negative frame. For example, oppressed followers question the toxic leader's motives (e.g., she is out to get me, he is only in this for the money) or abilities (e.g., he is incompetent, she does not understand how things work). The toxic leaders' behaviors suggest they do not

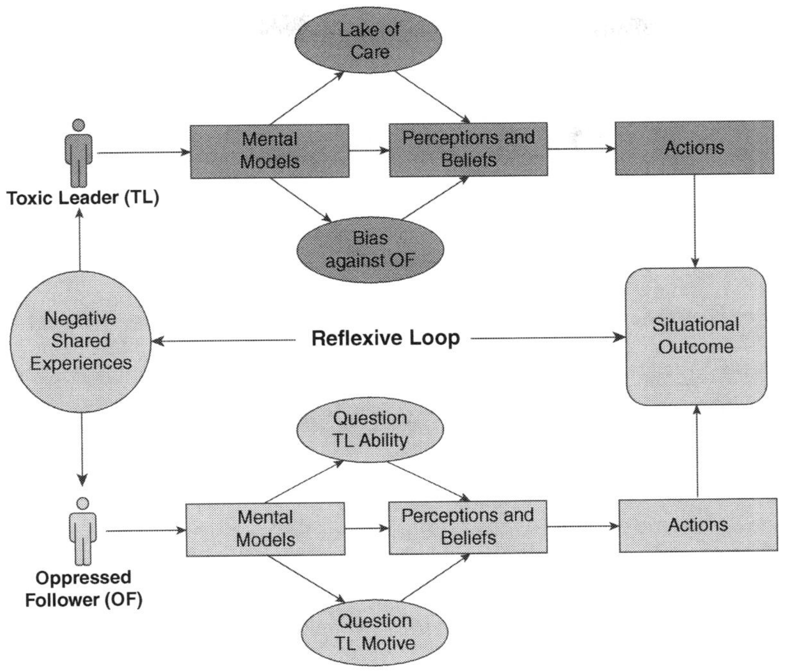

Figure 7.2 Closed system model of toxic leadership.

care about oppressed followers or do not trust their abilities to perform. The toxic leader's direct or indirect behavior then supports a continued cycle of slights, innuendo, undermining, under-resourcing, micromanaging, and complaints that work against the followers' abilities to perform. As each party acts based on their perceptions and beliefs, a vicious cycle is born in which adverse outcomes feed into new situations and shared experiences through a reflexive loop.

The toxic leader model depicted in Figure 7.2 is a closed system between the toxic leader and the oppressed follower(s). That model can be expanded into an open system when considering the organizational enablement of toxic leadership and the detrimental effects on oppressed followers (see Figure 7.3). The managers of toxic leaders may not have sufficient downward visibility into their organizations to understand that subordinates are toxic leaders. They might also have scorecards for their leaders that do not take human elements into account. As long as managers produce acceptable financial and operational outcomes, leaders might ignore other problems such as high turnover, negative 360-degree performance reviews, or personnel complaints. There might also be ambiguous signals from the subordinates of toxic leaders. Some followers of toxic leaders are not oppressed.

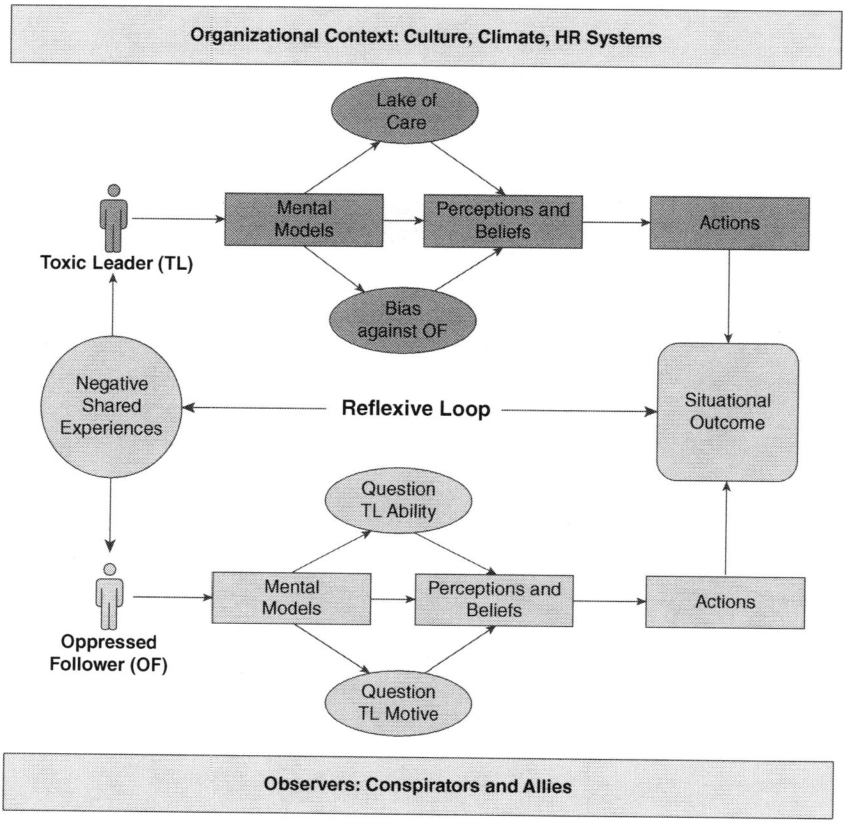

Figure 7.3 Open system model of toxic leadership.

Some followers receive beneficial effects from toxic leaders, while their colleagues suffer the toxic effects. For example, in a patriarchal organization, male subordinates of a toxic leader might benefit from the leader's toxic behaviors against their female peers.

Ideally, an employee could sit down with the leader and air any grievances. In that perfect world, both parties would listen carefully, present their evidence, learn from each other, and resolve the situation for mutual benefit. In reality, oppressed followers might have few options when working for toxic leaders. The toxic leader will have positional power and authority over the oppressed follower. Thus, the toxic leader will most likely have greater access to other organizational leaders and resources to suppress the follower further.

Institutional barriers, tenure, peer pressure, ignorance, and other factors may prevent oppressed followers from successfully navigating toxic situations. Human resource departments work to keep the organization from harm. Thus, HR representatives might side with the toxic leader over the oppressed follower, especially if the manager has already branded the employee as ineffective. HR might also be eager to prevent a toxic situation from turning into an opportunity for litigation. Thus, there might be an effort to "circle the wagons" to prevent the oppressed follower from gaining traction that could cast the organization in a negative light.

Executives might have many reasons to support their toxic leaders. They might doubt or be oblivious to organizational concerns. They might also believe toxic leaders' rhetoric, especially charismatic leaders who assure them that all is well. They might have friendships or affinities with toxic leaders that cloud their judgment or ability to assess the situation with impartiality. They might also fear that the toxic leader would sue the organization if fired.

Colleagues might also have reasons for dissuading action by an oppressed follower. They might disagree with the oppressed follower's assessment of the situation. The colleague might have reasons to prefer the status quo, such as maintaining privileged status. Some colleagues might not want to rock the boat for fear of being swept overboard themselves. Peers may also believe that oppressed colleagues are overplaying their concerns. They might commit the fundamental attribution error, believing that oppressed colleagues are targeted fairly rather than victims of toxic behaviors.

Followers might have many reasons for being unable or unwilling to fight back against toxic leaders. Followers might not have experienced constructive leadership. Some followers might be too inexperienced to understand whether leaders' behaviors are acceptable or out-of-bounds. Followers might not have the tenure or reach to have established positive relationships with influential leaders or peers. Thus, they might feel marooned, believing that others are unlikely to believe or support their grievances. Some followers might also be unaware of the organizational systems and processes designed to protect their interests. Followers also might have cultural or personal reasons for keeping quiet.

Implications

Based on the reasons given earlier, oppressed followers might feel that the cards are stacked against them. Indeed, the followers in this study rarely reported beneficial coping strategies. They were more likely to ride out the situation than act in their self-interest.

Followers

- Document the situation in detail with contemporaneous notes, dates, and facts. Keep the notes outside of organizational information systems and consider having a few copies.
- Develop political acumen within the organization. Understand how the company creates value, acceptable behaviors, political centers of power, and where is the toxic leader connected.

- Build coalitions to change the balance of power. For example, work on cross-departmental committees to build relationships with other leaders and peers. Build a strong reputation and a broad network of people who can attest to work ethic and output.
- Act professionally and maintain a strong work ethic. Do not fall into acting out against the organization through work slowdowns, tantrums, and gossip.
- Attempt to keep open lines of communication with the toxic leader by openly addressing concerns, if possible.
- Exercise caution when approaching human resources, understanding that they work for the organization and not for the employee. Always do so professionally and with a solid case. Seek outside legal counsel if necessary.
- Develop self-care routines to counter stress, burnout, and other harmful effects of the toxic situation.

Organization

Organizations need to be on the lookout for toxic leaders and toxic environments. The organization cannot assume that employees will report toxic leadership because of fear of reprisal. Therefore, the organization may need to create anonymous listening posts, feedback mechanisms, and exit briefings to receive candid feedback. The organization must also act fairly on feedback to build trust. HR representatives need to be trained to recognize toxic leadership, understand the effects, and provide counsel to employees affected by toxic leaders.

Colleagues must also consider stepping out of the shadows and reporting toxic leadership. It may take moral and intellectual courage to report bad behavior, especially in the face of possible repercussions. Therefore, organizations must make it safe for employees to call out toxic behaviors. Colleagues might also consider acting together to seek safety in numbers. Depending on the type of toxic leader, the oppressed follower and colleagues might consider intervening together with the toxic leader. For example, the oppressed follower and allies might approach a paternalistic leader to point out discriminatory behavior against women.

Some toxic leaders are morally corrupt. Others may be unaware of their biases against employees or how their poor leadership affects subordinates. Those who are ignorant or ineffective might change their behavior if the organization intervened or if the oppressed follower challenged the toxic leader effectively. Leaders can use the indicators listed in Table 7.6 as potential symptoms of a toxic environment. If some of these indicators are present, leaders should investigate further.

Table 7.6 Potential Signs of Toxic Leadership

Followers	*Organizational Climate*	*Organizational Outcomes*
Low commitment	Bad moods	High turnover
High stress	Everyone for themselves	Inefficiency
Low job satisfaction	Intentional social distancing	Low productivity
Anxiety	Divisiveness	Low growth
Depression	Low morale	High costs of recruitment
Disengagement	Distrust	High costs of retraining
Fear	Fear	Litigation
Stalled career development		
Physical health issues		
Mental health issues		
Loss of creativity		
Sleep deprivation		
Emotional exhaustion		
Cynicism		
Contempt		

References

Anjum, A., Ming, X., Siddiqi, A. F., & Rasool, S. F. (2018). An empirical study analyzing job productivity in toxic workplace environments. *International Journal of Environmental Research and Public Health*, *15*(5), 1035. https://doi.org/10.3390/ijerph15051035

Baloyi, G. T. (2020). Toxicity of leadership and its impact on employees: Exploring the dynamics of leadership in an academic setting. *HTS Teologiese Studies*, *76*(2), a5949. https://doi.org/10.4102/hts.v76i2.5949

Burns, W. A. (2021). A typology of destructive leadership: Pseudotransformational, laissez-faire, and unethical causal factors and predictors. In S. M. Camgöz & Ö. T. Ekmekci (Eds.), *Destructive leadership and management hypocrisy* (pp. 49–66). Emerald Publishing Limited. https://doi.org/10.1108/978-1-80043-180-520211004

Cote, R. (2018). Dark side leaders: Are their intentions benign or toxic? *Journal of Leadership, Accountability and Ethics*, *15*(2), 42–65.

Daft, R. (2014). *The leadership experience*. Cengage Publishing.

Dobbs, J. M. (2014). *The relationship between perceived toxic leadership styles, leader effectiveness, and organizational cynicism* [Dissertation, University of San Diego]. ProQuest Dissertations Publishing. https://go.exlibris.link/zr5KvJKs

Dobbs, J. M., & Do, J. J. (2019). The impact of perceived toxic leadership on cynicism in officer candidates. *Armed Forces & Society*, *45*(1), 3–26. https://doi.org/10.1177/0095327x17747204

Friedman, H., & Gerstein, M. (2017). Leading with compassion: The key to changing the organizational culture and achieving success. *Psychosociological Issues in Human Resource Management*, *5*(1), 160–175. https://doi.org/10.22381/pihrm5120175

Gabriel, J. M. O. (2016). Supervisors' toxicity as predictor of subordinates' counterproductive work behavior in Nigerian public hospitals. *Journal of Applied Business Research*, *32*(5), 1363–1374. https://doi.org/10.19030/jabr.v32i5.9765

Han, G. H., Harms, P. D., & Bai, Y. (2017). Nightmare bosses: The impact of abusive supervision on employees' sleep, emotions, and creativity. *Journal of Business Ethics, 145*(1), 21–31. https://doi.org/10.1007/s10551-015-2859-y

Hinshaw, S. (2019, November 13). Toxic leadership: My story. *Stephanie Hinshaw Blog*. www.stephaniehinshaw.com/post/toxic-leadership-my-story

Kendrick, K. D. (2017). The low morale experience of academic librarians: A phenomenological study. *Journal of Library Administration, 57*(8), 846–878. https://doi.org/10.1080/01930826.2017.1368325

Kets de Vries, M. F. R., & Miller, D. (1985). Narcissism and leadership: An object relations perspective. *Human Relations, 38*(6), 583–601. https://doi.org/10.1177/001872678503800606

Maamari, B. E., & Majdalani, J. F. (2017). Emotional intelligence, leadership style and organizational climate. *International Journal of Organizational Analysis, 2005, 25*(2), 327–345. https://doi.org/10.1108/IJOA-04-2016-1010

Maccoby, M. (2000). Narcissistic leaders: The incredible pros, the inevitable cons. *Harvard Business Review*, 69–77. https://hbr.org/2004/01/narcissistic-leaders-the-incredible-pros-the-inevitable-cons

Matos, K., O'Neill, O. M., & Lei, X. (2018). Toxic leadership and the masculinity contest culture: How "win or die" cultures breed abusive leadership. *Journal of Social Issues, 74*(3), 500–528. https://doi.org/10.1111/josi.12284

Mohiuddin, Z. (2017). Influence of leadership style on employees' performance: Evidence from literatures. *Journal of Marketing and Management, 8*(1), 18–30.

Nusair, D. (2019). Top 10 bad bosses in movies. *liveabout.com*. www.liveabout.com/bad-bosses-in-movies-2432060

Ong, C. W., Roberts, R., Arthur, C. A., Woodman, T., & Akehurst, S. (2016). The leader ship is sinking: A temporal investigation of narcissistic leadership. *Journal of Personality, 84*(2), 237–247. https://doi.org/10.1111/jopy.12155

Paltu, A., & Brouwers, M. (2020). Toxic leadership: Effects on job satisfaction, commitment, turnover intention and organisational culture within the South African manufacturing industry. *SA Journal of Human Resource Management, 18*. http://dx.doi.org/10.4102/sajhrm.v18i0.1338

Raskin, R., & Terry, H. (1988). A principal-components analysis of the narcissistic personality inventory and further evidence of its construct validity. *Journal of Personality and Social Psychology, 54*(5), 890–902. https://doi.org/10.1037/0022-3514.54.5.890

Rasool, G., Naseer, S., Syed, F., & Ahmad, I. (2018). Despotic leadership and employees' outcomes: Mediating effect of impression management. *Pakistan Journal of Commerce and Social Sciences, 12*(3), 784–806. http://hdl.handle.net/10419/193447

Rosenthal, S. A., & Pittinsky, T. L. (2006). Narcissistic leadership. *The Leadership Quarterly, 17*(6), 617–633. https://doi.org/10.1016/j.leaqua.2006.10.005

Schmidt, A. A. (2014). *An examination of toxic leadership, job outcomes, and the impact of military deployment* [Dissertation, University of Maryland]. ProQuest Dissertations Publishing.

Wegge, J., Shemla, M., & Haslam, S. A. (2014). Leader behavior as a determinant of health at work: Specification and evidence of five key pathways. *German Journal of Human Resource Management, 28*(1–2), 6–23. https://doi.org/10.1177/239700221402800102

Yasharoff, H. (2021, January 27). Two top CBS execs on leave after LA Times investigation alleged racist, misogynistic culture, reports say. *USA Today*. www.usatoday.com/story/entertainment/tv/2021/01/27/cbs-execs-leave-after-la-times-alleged-toxic-workplace/4273907001/

Zwerdling, D. (2014, January 6). Army takes on its own toxic leaders. *NPR*. www.npr.org/2014/01/06/259422776/army-takes-on-its-own-toxic-leaders

8 Aberrant Behavior Cases

Chapters 8–14 include several cases of toxic leadership. In these cases, we share oppressed followers' stories based on their experiences with toxic leaders. We "cleaned up" these testimonials to ensure anonymity; however, we retained the author's "voice", including spelling or grammar errors, to keep the tenor and tone of each story.

A toxic leader type forms the base for each ensuing chapter. We share a summary of the type, three or four supporting cases, a chapter summary, and sources cited. The cases consist of a testimonial, followed by four sets of questions.

1. Reflective journaling questions evoke thoughtful reflection, application to personal experiences, and extension to professional contexts.
2. Basic questions require the identification of connections within the chapter.
3. Advanced questions draw more broadly from the book material and require the application of critical thinking skills.
4. Questions for leaders will be helpful for organizational leaders to develop their abilities to recognize toxic leaders and lead culture and climate change efforts to eliminate toxic leadership.

Aberrant Behavior

We start with the *aberrant behavior* category. Aberrant behavior includes toxic leader qualities that reflect narcissism and paranoia. Narcissistic behaviors include repeated patterns of self-importance, an exaggerated belief in accomplishments, a demand for fealty from subordinates, and a lack of ability to empathize with subordinates. Paranoid behaviors include unfounded or unreasonable suspicion and holding a grudge.

Aberrant toxic leaders may or may not meet the clinical definitions of narcissistic personality disorder or paranoid personality disorder. They may exhibit some or even lower levels of the characteristics. Recall that a clinical diagnosis of narcissistic personality disorder relates to ongoing patterns of

DOI: 10.4324/9781003202462-8

grandiosity, need for admiration, and lack of empathy that must meet at least five of the following characteristics:

(a) These leaders have a grandiose sense of self-importance, exaggerate achievements and talents, or expect to be recognized as superior without commensurate achievements.
(b) These individuals are preoccupied with fantasies of unlimited success, power, brilliance, beauty, or ideal love.
(c) Narcissistic individuals believe that they are "special" and unique and can only be understood by, or should associate with, other special or high-status people or institutions.
(d) They require excessive admiration.
(e) They have a sense of entitlement, that is, unreasonable expectations of especially favorable treatment or compliance with their expectations.
(f) Individuals who have narcissistic personality disorder are interpersonally exploitive, taking advantage of others to achieve their ends.
(g) They also lack empathy and are unwilling to recognize or identify with the feelings and needs of others.
(h) They are often envious of others or believe that others are envious of them.
(i) Lastly, narcissistic individuals show arrogance, haughty behaviors, or attitudes. (American Psychiatric Press, 2000, p. 717)

Paranoid personality disorder relates to a repeated pattern of distrust and suspicion (American Psychiatric Press, 2000). As much as 2.5% of the US population suffers from paranoid personality disorder. People who have paranoid personality disorder must meet at least four of the following characteristics:

(a) They suspects, without sufficient basis, and believe that others are exploiting, harming, or deceiving them.
(b) They are preoccupied with unjustified doubts about the loyalty or trustworthiness of friends and associates.
(c) They are reluctant to confide in others because they believe the information given will be used against them later.
(d) They read hidden demeaning or threatening meanings into benign remarks or events.
(e) They persistently bear grudges, unforgiving of insults, injuries, or sights.
(f) They perceive attacks on their character or reputation that are not apparent to others and are quick to react angrily or counterattack.
(g) Paranoid individuals have recurrent suspicions, without justification, regarding the fidelity of their spouse or sexual partner. (American Psychiatric Press, 2000, p. 694)

Aberrant toxic leadership may lead to organizational outcomes such as high turnover, operational inefficiency, low productivity, low growth, increased recruitment costs, and retraining costs. The effects on oppressed followers and allies can be devastating. Followers suffer from stress, anxiety, depression, disengagement, fear, physical and mental health issues, and low job satisfaction and commitment.

The following four testimonials highlight aspects of aberrant toxic leadership.

Case 8.1

The Testimonial

My toxic boss always felt the need to brag about her finances, how well she was doing, and how rich she was. During the COVID-19 pandemic, many of us were hurting financially and struggling to make ends meet. At the start of every team meeting, my boss would begin by talking about how she had just bought an expensive house in a nice neighborhood, and how her and her husband were going to purchase a $50k motorcycle. She even goes as far to make comments about how her finances have never been better.

Meanwhile, the rest of us on her team are barely able to pay rent. Her bragging about how she is feasting during times of famine for the rest of us shows a lack of empathy toward the rest of her employees. She will also make fun of employees that mention they are struggling financially.

These behaviors that can be utilized by my employer are narcissistic as she is able to maintain a people person type of attitude around her boss, but changes when she is around her followers. The only time she exerts care and concern is when productivity of the shop and or income is lower than average. Even then she may ask why a person is slacking rather than if they are ok and or if they need to seek medical attention or go home early.

Impact on the Organizational Environment

When walking into work, there is a dense cloud of anxiety and uncertainty that hangs over the heads of each employee. The anxiety and uncertainty that overshadow us all brings a "walking-on-egg-shells" type mentality to the table, as we never know who we are going to get, Doctor Jekyll or Mr. Hyde. The animosity and tension can be cut with a dull knife.

An example, while walking into work I was greeted by my boss with a good morning how was your weekend. The following day I was greeted with, "what time is it?" My response was, "6:45 AM."

I was then harassed for the next hour about showing up 30 minutes early for work instead of 15 minutes. As an employee of hers, you never knew what you would get day to day.

Coping

One would say it isn't easy trying to work through the treatment along with the environment that is my work. I have had to resort to pulling out the thought process I lived with while in the military. It is more of a yes ma'am or no ma'am style of working, which allows me to get through the day. Even that tends to wear on a person when day in and day out the treatment is poor. The morale in our department is at an all-time low. Many of my fellow employees have suffered mental health problems. I had to start seeing a therapist and I have been put on medication for depression. Without these pills, the days would be bleak and the want to continue would be low.

Outcome

When it comes to a solution to this problem, it is simple, in order to regain my mental health, I must leave the organization and get away from this toxic leader. The fear of the unknown constantly weighs in as though I have a boulder on my chest. The question that haunts me is, am I making the right decision to leave, or should I stay and tough it out with my coworkers? We are all in charge of our own paths and we must act when our path begins to narrow. I have elected to move on. Last year when the pandemic hit, I decided I would achieve my MBA. Once I obtain my degree, I will be hunting for positions outside of my current industry to get a new start. This will allow me to focus on new challenges, which should in theory help me in the mental health department. The match has been struck, the flame is hot now to throw it on the gas, and move on.

Reflection Journal

We recommend you keep a journal to reflect and write, using these questions to prompt your thinking.

1. What were your immediate impressions of this testimonial?
2. Was there some experience that you have had that contributed to how you initially thought about this case?
3. Why did you develop these initial impressions?
4. Do you think that other followers in this organization share the concerns of this oppressed follower?

5. What sort of leadership is exhibited in this testimonial?
6. What are you reading into this situation?
7. What more would you want to know about this situation?

Basic Questions

1. What behaviors did the oppressed follower identify as toxic? Do you agree with this assessment?
2. What actions did the oppressed follower take to cope with the toxic leader?
3. Do you agree with the oppressed follower's claim that the toxic leader was a narcissist?

Advanced Questions

1. What coping strategies has this oppressed follower used in dealing with the toxic leader?
2. What evidence supports a psychological component to this case?
3. How would you characterize the culture or climate of this organization?
4. What advice would you give this employee on how to deal with this situation?

Questions for Leaders

1. How would you handle this situation if you received this information:
   a. In an anonymous letter?
   b. In an exit interview?
2. Could a similar situation exist in your organization without your knowledge?
3. Reflect on your impressions of how this follower conforms to your concept of an effective follower.

Case 8.2

It was supposed to be good news. I was getting promoted with a nice salary increase. However, with the promotion and pay increase came a new leader to report to. As soon as I was informed of this information, I was petrified. I was not sure if I should accept the promotion anymore. I was not sure of what to do. Part of me did not want to turn down this fantastic opportunity I had worked so hard for, but I was terrified of this new leader. The new leader I would report to was the type of supervisor that was narcissistic.

She was the type of leader that wanted all her employees and team to praise her constantly. She wanted her followers to believe that she was the best supervisor in the organization. She would tell us that we were lucky to have her as a leader. When our department did well, she took the credit. When our department was down, it was everyone else's fault but her own. She was starving for admiration from her team and everyone in the organization. Unfortunately, she lacked empathy for anyone.

I recall one of her followers was going through a nasty divorce. The divorce took an enormous toll on her, and it affected her work life. Before the divorce, this follower was number one in the department for opening credit, customer service, and was employee of the month. When this employee began struggling due to her divorce, the leader called her out in a team meeting in front of everyone. She pointed at her and yelled, "Leave your problems at home! Get back on track! Your performance ultimately makes ME look bad! Do you understand that?!" This was just one of many examples.

Environment

The environment became so toxic that some employees would call out of their shift or asked to be transferred to other departments. We would sometimes hide from her because every time she would talk to us it was always a negative experience. Whenever anyone could not meet their goal for the week, she would call them out in front of the team, saying they were useless and worthless. She would threaten us with termination.

Coping

I coped with this leader in several ways. The first one was through a formal complaint to human resources, which ended up going nowhere. This toxic leader was great at being charming to those above her, but when it came to her employees, she would change into someone completely different. The second way I tried to cope was to have a stronger state of mind so I would not allow her to affect me personally and psychologically. Fortunately, this leader finally moved on to another position at another company. A day after she left, the organizational environment changed dramatically. It was like everyone could breathe again. I am happy to report that the new leader is much better. This new leader created a more supportive and relational environment. Morale is much improved, and our productivity has increased significantly.

Reflection Journal

We recommend you keep a journal to reflect and write, using these questions to prompt your thinking.

1. Have you experienced a change of supervisor in which the new supervisor had a dramatically different style from your previous supervisor?
2. Did your new supervisor take time to build trust in the group?
3. Did your new supervisor take time to understand the culture of the organization?
4. Have you been promoted or hired into an organization where you were concerned about your new supervisor's reputation?
5. How did your new supervisor act to either support or ease your concerns?
6. What is the obligation of the oppressed followers, allies, or other organizational actors to take a strong stance against the behaviors of toxic leaders?
7. Does this obligation line up with how things work in the real world?

Basic Questions

1. Which behaviors line up with narcissistic personality disorder characteristics?
2. What were some of the organizational outcomes that resulted from the toxic leader's behavior?
3. What actions did the oppressed follower take to cope with the toxic leader?

Advanced Questions

1. Does the testimonial support a clinical diagnosis of narcissistic personality disorder?
2. Should the followers of this toxic leader have combined their voices to amplify their complaints about this leader?
3. What organizational systems failed the employee in this case?

Questions for Leaders

1. What is a leader's responsibility to craft an image of approachability? In other words, should a leader ensure that followers or potential followers are not afraid to approach the leader?
2. What is an appropriate response for a leader when an employee's performance suffers because of a personal issue (e.g., divorce)?
3. How can organizational systems be designed to protect employees while still respecting due process and the company's interests?
4. The oppressed follower stated that morale and productivity improved after the toxic leader left the company. How might the organization learn from the situation?
5. How would you react if someone confided this story with you and the toxic leader was still in the organization?

Case 8.3

When I worked as a student employee in a large financial company during my bachelor's degree in Berlin, I worked for a narcissistic leader for a while. What was striking was that he initially had many positive attributes at first. He made a very sympathetic, nice, and professional impression at the beginning, especially to those above him. At that time, I was already rather surprised that many employees who had been with the company for a longer time made negative comments about his leadership style. After some time, I also noticed these narcissistic traits, which greatly impacted the entire organizational environment. He used a highly developed self-presentation style and had a strong sense of self-esteem. He was also extremely self-centered, which made team communication and teamwork very difficult. He put a lot of pressure on the team, and everyone worked very hard to achieve the goals he set. Unfortunately, when the team would reach the goals or overachieve, he would take all the credit, and when we missed the goals, he blamed everyone but himself. This demotivated the entire team. After a few months, the team morale was low, and our productivity suffered.

Environment

The organizational atmosphere was very negative and toxic. The commitment and the motivation for innovation decreased due to him attributing any positive success to himself. When mistakes were made or the numbers went down, he had emotional outbursts and always looked for the mistakes in others. One could not communicate openly with him about problems.

Outcome

The result was that, although the company and the job itself were very exciting, I decided not to work in this company any longer after receiving my college degree. Higher management was, unfortunately, more focused on the numbers and successes my boss was achieving than listening to his followers and questioning his narcissism and the plethora of complaints. Although some employees spoke out against him, no consequences were implemented. From my own experience, it can be said that it is difficult to oppose and directly confront a narcissistic personality. The reason for this is often, as it was in my case, that the narcissist has already one over upper leadership, so they will not listen to the lower-level employees.

What Should Be Done?

Unfortunately, there are many successful companies with a high number of toxic leaders. Organizations, leaders, and HR should take more responsibility and act. They need to listen more to their employees, and more frequently take a critical look at their own leaders to see whether they are acting according to the right values of the company and in the interests of their employees. In my opinion, this is the only way a company can achieve long-term success and retain good talent.

Reflection Journal

We recommend you keep a journal to reflect and write, using these questions to prompt your thinking.

1. Do organizations have to choose between focus on people and focus on profits?
2. Can organizations successfully balance the polarity between people and profits?
3. Have you met people who initially appeared to have many positive qualities that you later determined to be a show?
4. Have you worked with a supervisor who seemed to have a different way of being in front of supervisors than with subordinates?
5. What are some of the difficulties of overcoming toxic situations in which the toxic leader appears to have snowed the people above?

Basic Questions

1. Which behaviors line up with narcissistic personality disorder characteristics?
2. Did any behaviors line up with paranoid personality disorder?
3. What were some of the organizational outcomes that resulted from the toxic leader's behavior?
4. What actions did the oppressed follower take to cope with the toxic leader?

Advanced Questions

1. What could this student employee have done change their experience into a more productive opportunity?
2. What can leaders do to ensure their employees know that they are advocating for them and giving them credit for their work?
3. What sort of climate would you say this organization exhibits?
4. Is there enough evidence to describe the organizational culture?

Questions for Leaders

1. Is it disrespectful or inappropriate for leaders to engage with subordinates who are a few levels below them in the chain of command?
2. How should leaders handle complaints related to their subordinate managers or supervisors?
3. Would it be ok to demand that individuals attempt to work things out with their boss before jumping the chain of command?
4. How would you ensure that individuals do not exercise inappropriate forms of power over student employees or volunteer?

Case 8.4

Within the 2015–2020 timeframe, my department experienced toxic leadership from the director level. The current organizational structure is different now, but at the time the director was four levels above me within the chain of command. The toxic behaviors displayed by the director included a lack of respect and a lack of empathy for the workers. During one of my first interactions with the toxic leader, they literally said to me, "I'm working on my empathy." Needless to say, this seemed like a red flag to me, but I gave them the benefit of the doubt at that time.

During an all-hands meeting for my department, many workers provided sincere and heartfelt concerns about the changes in the direction of the department. In response to their concerns, the director became upset and very defensive. The director was unable to accept that they could possibly be doing something wrong. Tensions grew within the room as more workers expressed their feelings of anxiety and unease about upcoming changes. As the level of tension grew within the meeting, the director eventually had enough and told us, "If you don't like it, the door is right there. You don't even have to badge out." (Our campus requires a company-issued badge to access doors on-site for security reasons.) Instead of reassuring and understanding the workers, we were met with hostility and fear. This director lacked the empathy to deal with the reactions to change. As one could imagine, the meeting went downhill very quickly after that comment. The last smidgen of trust was utterly destroyed, and this effectively sealed the director's fate. That "leader" was gone within a few months.

Environment

The organizational environment left behind is that of palpable distrust between the workers and upper management. The new director and associate director have yet to acknowledge the errors of the past regime, so the culture within the department remains in a state of confused limbo. Many of the workers feel apathetic toward the workplace and feel dissatisfied with their jobs. There continues to be uncertainty regarding the future of the department, and many people still wonder if they are going to lose their jobs to an outsourced agency. People are afraid to speak their minds and challenge the status quo for fear of reprimand. The "speak-up" environment that management hopes to achieve remains a dream until the underlying issues are fixed.

The past director had already enacted some changes (before they left) and the department is still reeling from the negative effects to this day. One of the changes was letting go of all the middle management. Another change was bringing in an outside agency to share our workload. The lack of proper change management has left the workers to fend for themselves and discover/experience the effects of change without leadership.

Coping

Most people coped with toxic leadership by submission. Most were afraid of losing their job, so they kept their heads down and continued performing their day-to-day tasks as normal. I coped with the situation by taking more paid time off than I usually would. As a silver lining to this experience, I have developed a greater appreciation for vacation time. There is a very real importance to balancing work and leisure, and it took a toxic environment to help me realize that I have been sacrificing my home life needlessly.

Another coping mechanism is my drive to work harder and rise to the challenge. I have noted the lack of leadership (not management) within my department, and this need has finally given me the last push to start my Master's in Organizational Leadership. To fill the void of leadership, I am fully expecting to grow in the form of behavioral change and a shift in my mindset.

Conclusions

Experiencing a toxic leader first-hand was a learning opportunity. I know what I don't want in a leader. I continue to learn what I don't want, and I expect to never stop learning during my leadership journey. Although I did not see all six of the toxic typologies, I only knew that director for a year. There's much work to do regarding healing the department, and I think it has to start with trust and dialogue. I think the human aspect of leadership has been ignored for too long because of all the changes, new complex processes, and the loss of middle management. Since I believe I have a general understanding of what is going wrong with the department, my challenge is to grow myself enough to change the department for the better.

Reflection Journal

We recommend you keep a journal to reflect and write, using these questions to prompt your thinking.

1. The director invited people to leave the organization if they were not happy with the direction of change. How would you characterize that interaction?
2. Does a higher organizational level equate to a greater right to be in a company? In other words, should higher-level people be able to tell subordinates that if they don't like things they can hit the highway?
3. What would happen if the subordinates turned the tables and invited the director to quit if they comfortable dealing with the collective concerns?
4. Have you ever witnessed a contentious meeting like the one described in the testimonial?

Basic Questions

1. Does this organization seem to have a hierarchical or a flat organizational structure?
2. What elements of narcissism or paranoia were evident in this case?
3. What were the coping mechanisms displayed by the oppressed follower?
4. What were the outcomes of the toxic leader's behaviors?

Advanced Questions

1. Explain how the supervisor's claim about working on their empathy is both an encouraging sign and a potential red flag.
2. Describe how the director's actions lacked empathy for the employees expressing their concerns about the changes.
3. What questions do you feel need to be answered about this case?

Questions for Leaders

1. How should a leader handle a meeting where they feel attacked by staff members who are resisting a change initiative?
2. The director reportedly said, "If you don't like it, the door is right there. You don't even have to badge out." Explain whether this statement was problematic or not.
3. As a lower-level leader, what would you tell your subordinates who were at meeting in which someone above you in the organizational hierarchy made that statement?
4. As a leader in the company, would you have a responsibility to talk to Human Resources about the director's statement?

5. What leadership development tools or interventions might help leaders to develop their levels of empathy?
6. How should the new director and associate director handle this situation? Should they "acknowledge the errors of the past regime?"

Reference

American Psychiatric Press. (2000). *Diagnostic and statistical manual of mental disorders – DSM-IV-TR*. American Psychiatric Press.

9 Abuse of Power Cases

Abuse of Power

For Baloyi (2020), toxic leadership consists of the abuse and degradation of employees. This type of toxic leadership includes leaders who abuse authority positions by consistently degrading employees, ridiculing employees in public, forcing employees to undergo physical and psychological pain, and promoting divisiveness between colleagues (Baloyi, 2020). These leaders create environments of low morale, stress, anxiety, depression, distrust, fear, high turnover, everyone for themselves culture, low growth, low motivation, and an increase in litigation on their firms.

The following four testimonials demonstrate abuse of power.

Case 9.1

The Testimonial

This toxic leader is the manager of a pharmacy I worked at. He would regularly berate the male employees and show favoritism toward the younger and more attractive female employees. One incident I remember; I was working in inventory and auditing the controlled medications. My coworker "Jim" was working with the dispensing machine, while "Mary" was just learning it and assisting him. Jim was doing a great job. I knew this because I went through advanced training with the manufacturer so I could teach all the other employees how to use and maintain the machine. Mary was complaining about how difficult it was. Our leader came over to check on us, as he always did (he was particularly fond of micromanaging).

"Hey, Andrew! Stop inventory and help this dummy over here with the machine!" He yelled. Then he turned to Mary, "Mary, you are awesome, go take a break sweetie," He would use various "cute"

DOI: 10.4324/9781003202462-9

nicknames for the female employees while shouting at the males. I told him I wasn't done yet and he glared at me and yelled I could finish it later. I went to help Jim and told him he was doing well, after the manager walked out of hearing distance.

Environment

The degradation and ridicule were constant and came in the form of shouting and insults toward the male employees. The environment became divisive, stressful, and our morale plummeted. The divisiveness came from the different treatment between males and females. The different treatment between the genders from him made the males resentful toward him and the females.

Coping

This manager thought he was funny. His idea of jokes was insults randomly yelled at male employees about how they looked, their weight, or even small things like what kind of car they drove. No one thought he was funny but everyone would fake laugh so he wouldn't be in a bad mood. That is how most of the employees often coped with many of his behaviors. By agreeing with him, we were enabling his behaviors, but also avoiding the consequences of disagreeing. Some would employ the tactic of completely avoiding him or pretending they didn't hear him. Personally, I began having major anxiety issues. After a while I could no longer cope. Eventually, near the end of my employment there, I had a severe panic attack. Not the manager, but corporate, suggested that I take an extended leave. The extended leave led to me deciding to leave the job because of leader's blatant abuse.

Reflection Journal

We recommend you keep a journal to reflect and write, using these questions to prompt your thinking.

1. Sometimes, isolated behaviors do not seem abusive. Instead, only in retrospect might the pattern of behaviors take shape as abuse. In such a case, it may be difficult for bystanders to recognize or act on the behaviors they see. At some point, people will start to think that certain behaviors are abusive, and they will form opinions. Have you observed

isolated incidents that you later attributed to a pattern of abusive behaviors in your workplace?
2. How difficult is it to hold someone accountable for their abusive behaviors?
3. Does laughing at a person's jokes and insults to get along make one complicit in the behavior?
4. A polarity refers to a situation in which two contradictory choices must be balanced to achieve success. For example, organizations must also balance the need for strict controls over acceptable behaviors and allowing employees the freedom to act. Strict controls protect the organization and vulnerable employees from abuse. On the other hand, strict controls may also make employees afraid to act naturally. People might not tolerate working at a company whose controls are too strict. They might be subject to toxic behaviors if controls are not strict enough. What polarities do you see in this situation?

Basic Questions

1. Which elements the pharmacy manager's behavior were toxic?
2. What were some of the adverse effects of the pharmacy manager's behavior?
3. What were organizational outcomes of the pharmacy manager's behaviors?

Advanced Questions

1. Assess the effectiveness of the followers' behaviors?
2. Did the followers support each other in dealing with the toxic pharmacy manager?
3. Was the corporate action to recommend that the oppressed follower take extended leave in the best interests of the employee?

Questions for Leaders

1. Who is responsible for improving this situation?
2. Do the employees in this situation appear to have power to stand up for themselves?
3. What actions might they take to develop their power?
4. Was the pharmacy manager's behavior illegal?
5. What organizational systems seem to allow the pharmacy manager to get away with toxic behaviors?
6. How should the corporate office respond to employee complaints about their manager's abusive behaviors?

Case 9.2

Testimonial

A previous supervisor of mine was new to the organization at the time, but I knew this person from a previous organization that we had both worked at. This individual had been passed over for a promotion due to him being written up multiple times for misconduct including harsh verbal treatment of his employees. This event prompted him to seek other employment opportunities in which he became my supervisor.

To those who did not work daily with this supervisor this person was seen as highly charismatic, humorous, and a strong leader. Hidden in the day-to-day office interactions were an incessant demand for respect, and constant displays of power through degrading and humiliating his employees. Employees, including myself, feared speaking to someone in a higher position about his actions out of fear he would retaliate. Our team only consisted of five people, so it was almost certain he would pinpoint which person made the complaint and retaliate against them.

Environment

There are two examples I will share that highlight his abuse of power and the environment of fear he created. The first example had to do with a parking space. I arrive to work an hour before my supervisor, and one morning, after my supervisor arrived, I was asked to come outside and look at how I parked my car. There I was shown that my tire was about two inches onto the yellow line of the parking spot. This was followed by him yelling at me for twenty minutes in the middle of the parking lot about how I was a loser, unprofessional, and did not take my work seriously. After being berated for the twenty minutes I finally had a chance to speak and let my supervisor know that when I pulled into the parking spot, I was accommodating the car of a client that was parked next to me over the line, to give them space to move their car I did not hug the line. This explanation was not sufficient, and I was again verbally reprimanded for not checking to see when this client had left so I could re-park my car. He yelled a few profanities at me and said if he saw me park unacceptably again, I would be fired on the spot.

The second scenario was when I clocked out at 3:58 pm instead of 4:00 pm one afternoon. The next morning, I was asked to meet in my supervisor's office where I was questioned if I wanted to keep my job or not, I was told that this type of work was not for everyone, and that by my actions I am demonstrating that I have no regard for my place of employment or the work we do.

Coping and Outcome

I regret to say that these events and other very vulgar language used against me caused me to leave this specific role in my place of employment for an opportunity in another department with a different leader. In one sense I regret not saying anything, in another sense I am grateful I was able to avoid this conflict that may have cost me my place of employment, which is vital for me to be financially stable. My coping mechanism for this specific incident was to find a way to escape to another department. This toxic leadership style of abusing power bred fear, distrust, and anxiety in the workplace. Since I switched departments, turnover in his area has been significant. All the employees I worked with have quit. What I hear about the department now is that the morale is low, and employees are stressed.

Reflection Journal

We recommend you keep a journal to reflect and write, using these questions to prompt your thinking.

1. The oppressed follower mentioned that employees "feared speaking to someone in a higher position about his actions out of fear he would retaliate," and they regretted "not saying anything." What can you infer about the company culture or climate that employees did not feel safe to speak out?
2. Have you been in a situation where you chose to move on rather than take a stand against an abusive leader? In retrospect, was there anything you could have done differently?
3. If employees are not speaking out against an abusive supervisor, how can the organization learn about the behavior and take action?
4. What are some warning signs that an abusive leader is mistreating employees?

Basic Questions

1. Which actions were abusive in this situation?
2. How did the oppressed follower cope with the situation?
3. What were the outcomes of the situation?

Advanced Questions

1. How would you characterize the culture of the organization?
2. How would you characterize the climate of the organization?
3. What options did the oppressed follower have besides moving to a different department?

Questions for Leaders

1. Is it problematic that the organization hired a manager who had a reputation for misconduct and being passed over for promotion?
2. Why would the manager have been seen as "highly charismatic, humorous, and a strong leader" to people outside of the unit?
3. What actions can leaders take to ensure that managers are not mistreating their employees?
4. What can leaders do to ensure that employees feel empowered to report mistreatment or bad behavior?
5. In your organization, do you have mechanisms to monitor climate, turnover, and engagement?

Case 9.3

Testimonial

One of the most prominent characteristics of toxic leaders is the abuse of power that surfaces in the abuse and degradation of the employees in a workplace. The behavior involves leaders manipulating control areas for individual gain at the employees' expense and avoiding fundamental managerial responsibility(s). I will refer to this leader as "Mr. X". Mr. X seemingly invented different ways to exploit people in every opportune circumstance. Some of the man's behaviors included ridiculing the juniors in public of ne'er-do-well issues and promoting divisiveness amongst the employees to further his agenda quickly. He was constantly inflicting psychological pain, especially with his heaps of insults and degradation. The female employees, who suffered the most as X kept stereotyping them for their inability to compete against men. There were instances when he would threw things at people and threaten to beat them up, especially if they stood against his way in most of the decisions. The result was bitter employees who lived out of fear of being on the wrong side of the manager, who seemed to (rather did) hold our jobs in his hands.

Environment

Toxic leadership leads to an environment that most likely makes it unbearable for the employees to survive. People lose confidence in themselves, especially if a leader abuses his or her power. It was evident in the organization – lack of appreciation no matter how we tried our best led to lowered self-esteem in whatever we did, as it was apparent it would be received with insults and ridicule. Low self-esteem also drops the morale to perform better. Humans appreciate a little praise from the seniors. The environment might turn toxic for the psychology of the employees, with cases of stress, anxiety, depression, distrust, and fear. Leaders who abuse power would generally have accomplices who stay awake to check on any form of mutiny from the others.

Coping

Sometimes, the leaders ensure no one knows who the spies are, which results in distrust amongst the employees and most likely will affect unity. Constant abuse and ridicule will affect the mental health of the victim, creating an environment of fear. The result is high turnover, as some people cannot exist in such toxic environments, which the company started experiencing. Lack of motivation and morale coupled with the high turnover led to the company's slurred growth, as reflected in the profit indices. The reign of terror indeed led to a plummeting business that threatened bankruptcy for the organization.

Contrary to his decisions, we decided not to feed his ego on whatever demons he woke with but focused on improving our skills and performing better. We agreed to always stand in solidarity and started boycotting and picketing work, especially if he became abusive toward our colleagues. After that, things became more burdensome, and we threatened him with disciplinary action from the board of management, which he had cunningly kept at bay, but for the poor financial performance of the organization. We were ready to make the scenes uglier by reporting to the police and seek legal intervention. Every time X decided to go out of his way, we would revoke the constitution, luckily, which he had no power. The short-lived age of terror made it possible and clear for us to understand the importance of workers' rights.

It has always been clear, every man has a breaking point, and Mr. X's was just around the corner. Soon, no one was giving in to his demands. Slowly, the employees began gaining their confidence and started working harder and better. Mr. X felt threatened as no one no longer felt the intimidation. It was hard for him to impose his terror on the workers.

Nevertheless, the company had suffered quite a loss, especially losing some of the most productive employees. We further moved on to impeach Mr. X. We ensured that we instituted more robust policies on the organization's constitution that would staff their leadership and impede any other case that would result in X's reign. Employees need to ensure they stay woke to reduce instances of toxic behavior from the management in the workplace.

Reflection Journal

We recommend you keep a journal to reflect and write, using these questions to prompt your thinking.

1. The testimonial spoke to the concept of worker rights. Do you agree that employers should be obligated to provide certain rights to their employees? What sort of rights do you think that all employees should claim?
2. Have you worked with a supervisor who seemed to pit employees against each other? Can you think of positive and negative aspects of this managerial style?
3. The testimonial speaks to the power of collective action. When employees lose trust in their managers, they may react by pulling together to resist the abusive behavior. Does it seem like the employees' collective action was effective in this situation?
4. What are your thoughts on employee unions? In your view, what are two to three key upsides and two to three key downsides to unions.

Basic Questions

1. What was the abusive behavior in this case?
2. How did the oppressed follower cope with the situation?
3. What were the outcomes of the situation?

Advanced Questions

1. Was there evidence of reprisal by the abusive manager?
2. Was this an ideal outcome, based on the situation?
3. What more would you expect to see from the employees in this situation?

Questions for Leaders

1. Did you see evidence that leadership was involved in solving this problem?
2. How would you characterize the employee's decision to work together to resolve their grievances with the abusive supervisor?
3. The oppressed follower mentioned that the employees were ready to seek assistance from law enforcement or the legal system. How would that have affected the situation?
4. How would your organization react if a group of employees sought collective relief from police or attorneys?
5. How would your answer change based on whether the employees had first placed a formal grievance with the organization?
6. What formal systems should be in place to ensure that employee grievances are heard, investigated, and adjudicated fairly?

Case 9.4

Testimonial

Being a 911 dispatcher is a tough career. I average 200 phone calls in an eight-hour period. I answer a range of calls, such as from people drunk in public, kids being lost, car accidents, and even prank calls. I have a very stressful job. The absolute last thing I need is a direct supervisor that doesn't fairly supervise all the employees.

In 2007, I started dispatching for a new Sheriff's department. I knew going into the job that the work conditions would be grueling. The station was undergoing a remodel, the city police department just merged with the Sheriff, and the city had a recent spike in crime. The dispatching room was relocated to a cramped office with no windows and barely enough room to accommodate all the 911 dispatchers. We were basically stuffed in a closet, answering priority calls back-to-back. My first call was about a deputy involved in a fight at a local bar. I was being yelled at by the witness on the 911 line, my co-dispatchers, and my supervisor, Deputy L.

Deputy L had been a supervisor of dispatchers for over ten years. She was known for her level-head and ability to bring out the best in her employees. If you were her favorite or her friend, it was great for you. If you fell on the other side, like I did and most others, good luck.

Deputy L openly criticized employees, not for their handling of the dispatch calls, but for the assignment of the calls to certain deputies in the field. She wanted her friends to get the easy calls and the deputies she wasn't friends with to get the more difficult calls. As dispatchers, you are trained to assign certain calls to trainees for them to gain experience and the rest are distributed to available deputies on duty. The way you gained L's favor was to bring her a Venti Chai Latte with Almond Milk at the beginning of the shift and that pretty much solidified your easy day as a patrol deputy. Deputy L would reassign radio calls to certain deputies after a dispatcher initially assigned them. She would yell out "reassign tag 212 to the rookie on the southside", knowing they were clear across town just so her friend didn't have to handle it.

Her behavior was very frustrating. She would invite her friends to extended lunches and cut our lunch short so we could handle the phones. Deputy L and her favorites would then return from these outings and discuss them in length while we are trying to handle emergent phone calls. The dispatch environment was a mess.

I can recall another incident when Deputy L was held over for an additional eight-hour shift and was told to draft two additional dispatchers. I was not next on the rotational draft list and she did it anyway. Two other dispatchers volunteered to take my spot, but she refused and made me work. She knew I had plans that day and I was looking forward to it. She also knew that if I didn't comply I could face disciplinary action. I held it together the entire shift. As I drove away with tears rolling down my face, I vowed to never speak again about my outside plans knowing that information could be used against me in the near future.

Environment

The environment around the dispatch room was thick with anxiety and stress. I always felt like I was walking on eggshells. We were never able to speak freely. Everyone did their best to avoid contact with Deputy L, as it was better to stay off her radar. You never knew when she was going to lash out or who would be her next victim of ridicule. As I think back over my time serving as a dispatcher there, I can feel my breathing being restricted. I started seeing a therapist as a result of me working that assignment.

Coping

After completing my one-year certification of 911 dispatcher, I began to look for other stations to work at for the Sheriff's Department. I went on seven different interviews. I prayed that some other station would pick me. Any place had to be better than where I was. During all those interviews, I knew I was doing a good job. I couldn't understand why I would get that follow up call saying they didn't choose me. A few months later, I found out Deputy L was being contacted directly from all the stations I interviewed with. She would tell them that I wasn't reliable and that I wouldn't be a good fit at their unit. I was furious. However, I didn't want to confront her because it would have ended poorly for me. I went on another interview and finally got picked for the new assignment. I was overwhelmed with delight as I would finally be free of her toxicity. My last night was a Sunday, 10 pm – 6am. It was a particularly busy night. The phones were ringing the entire shift. It was finally 6 a.m. and I was gathering my belongings to leave for my days off. As I turned to leave, Deputy L yelled out, "Smalls, you start your new assignment in two hours". I didn't believe her at all. She got her last jab at me. She then produced a folded-up paper that stated my release date was sent over ten days prior. I could do nothing but cry heavy tears all the way home.

Outcome

Months after I left that assignment, I heard from several of my former co-dispatchers that they transferred to other stations. A new captain was assigned to the station, and he made a lot of changes. Deputy L was sent to Tactical Communications and Cultural Awareness training. She was also transferred to the field where she handled the kind of radio calls she used to reassign. She was never promoted to a rank above deputy and has since retired from the Sheriff's Department.

Reflection Journal

We recommend you keep a journal to reflect and write, using these questions to prompt your thinking.

1. As a new employee in a new environment, it may take a while to understand the culture of an organization. This may make it difficult to recognize acceptable norms and customs. It can also be difficult to speak out against unacceptable norms. What role should senior individuals play in helping new members to understand the organizational culture?
2. Abusive supervisors will often attempt to isolate their subordinates from organizational support systems. Such actions might keep oppressed followers from accessing support or mentorship. How might organizations create a safe environment for new organizational members to enculturate and develop connections?

3. Social identity theory (Tajfel, 1974) and social comparison theory (Turner et al., 1979) hold that social interactions will be characterized by in-groups and out-groups (Wang et al., 2018). Within organizations, leadership is differentiated by in-group and out-group affiliation. Leaders provide more resources and give core assignments to in-group members. Conversely, they withhold resources and give routine and support tasks to out-group members. Social derogation suggests that familiarity with the same group or intergroup conflict results in outcomes such as derogatory stereotypes, differential pay, bias, and non-cooperation (Turner et al., 1979). Given the implications of social identity and social comparison theories, how might organizations overcome these natural tendencies?

Basic Questions

1. What was the abusive behavior in this case?
2. How did the oppressed follower cope with the situation?
3. What were the outcomes of the situation?

Advanced Questions

1. What was the climate of the dispatch room?
2. Was there evidence of group polarization, in-group favoritism, or out-group derogation?
3. Did the Sherriff's Department have an effective onboarding process?

Questions for Leaders

1. It is natural for people to develop an affinity toward certain people and groups. How does a leader keep from showing favoritism?
2. How does a leader ensure that small personal gestures (e.g., bringing a supervisor's favorite coffee drink) does not turn into favoritism or lead to a perception of favoritism?
3. Does a leader have an obligation to explicitly state that people will be treated fairly and respectfully, independent of the personal feelings of the leader?
4. Did the supervisor put the organization at risk by providing negative reference checks when the oppressed follower was looking for a new job?
5. Did the station leadership fail the dispatchers?
6. Are you aware of in-groups and out-groups within your own organization?
7. What can you do as a leader to decrease the negative effects of out-group affiliation on members in your organization?

References

Baloyi, G. T. (2020). Toxicity of leadership and its impact on employees: Exploring the dynamics of leadership in an academic setting [article]. *HTS Teologiese Studies/ Theological Studies*, *76*(2), e1–e8. https://doi.org/10.4102/hts.v76i2.5949

Tajfel, H. (1974). Social identity and intergroup behaviour. *Social Science Information*, *13*(2), 65–93. https://doi.org/10.1177/053901847401300204

Turner, J. C., Brown, R. J., & Tajfel, H. (1979). Social comparison and group interest ingroup favouritism. *European Journal of Social Psychology*, *9*(2), 187–204. https://doi.org/10.1002/ejsp.2420090207

Wang, L., Cheng, M. Y., & Wang, S. (2018). Carrot or stick? The role of in-group/ out-group on the multilevel relationship between authoritarian and differential leadership and employee turnover intention. *Journal of Business Ethics*, *152*(4), 1069–1084. https://doi.org/10.1007/s10551-016-3299-z

10 Egocentric Cases

Egocentrism

Chapter 10 will discuss the category of *egocentrism*. Piaget described egocentrism as the "tendency for children to perceive the world solely from their own perspective and to be unaware that other people may have different perspectives" (Schaffer, 2006, section: Egocentrism and Centration). Children develop the ability to see and empathize with different perspectives. Yet, some people develop more slowly, exhibiting egocentric behavior well into adolescence. We refer to egocentric leaders as focused on their points of view with little regard for other perspectives.

Egocentric leadership styles impact overall employee health, wellness, creativity, and productivity (Han et al., 2017; Rasool et al., 2018; Wegge et al., 2014). Matos et al. (2018) also found that egocentric leaders who demonstrated greed, selfishness, and hypocrisy caused subordinates to hold negative views of the organization and exhibit decreased well-being and self-worth.

The following three testimonials highlight aspects of egocentric toxic leadership.

Case 10.1

Testimonial

In the military, it is common to have to stand duty, which is a collateral job that requires more of your personal time to ensure the safety, security, and effectiveness of the unit you are at. At my current unit, the duty involves standing sentry; this is the physical security of the base over a 24-hour period. The job in itself is not very physically demanding but does mean there will be a lack of sleep, and due to the way it is set up, it is not abnormal to stand six days a month. Over

DOI: 10.4324/9781003202462-10

the summer, which is transfer season for the Coast Guard, people are spread increasingly thinner as we have fewer physical bodies to help fill the rotation. To mitigate this and the fatigue from burnout, I went to the Chief, the person in charge, and provided a solution that would involve pulling from the people who do not stand any duty as a temporary solution. Instead of being welcomed with a positive response, I was met with blank stares and confusion as to why I would even bring this up. I explained my concern for the safety of the members as, on a 24-hour watch, sleep is not in abundance. The exact response I got from this was, "suck it up; it's hard for everyone". Clearly, this response is never something you want to hear when you are looking out for the well-being of everyone, but when I take a step back and remember the type of person I am dealing with, it is almost predictable.

An egocentric person looks out for themselves, and the well-being of others is not even considered. The pushback largely comes from the fact that this Chief doesn't stand any duty, and my plan to help even for a small amount of time would require this Chief to contribute. Why would a person only looking out for themselves make a change that does not benefit them in any way? The answer here is that they wouldn't, and as assumed, she didn't. She acts out of selfishness, greed, and a complete lack of compassion for what she is putting others through. She makes people feel like they can bring up solutions, but instead of really considering if they would benefit the whole, her concern is how can it benefit me, or is there and negative personal impact?

Environment

Everyone learned very quickly there was no winning with this leader, and she would do everything she could to put the blame back on the junior members. This created a very uneasy and nervous environment for everyone underneath her. There was no trust and no motivation to work hard for this individual, especially when you knew they were only looking out for themselves.

When trying to deal with the nature of this Chief, it was reported to the command what has been happening, and she was counseled for her actions. Following the counseling, she came back to the group and stated, "you do not have the right to feel uneasy around me"! If red flags were not going up before, they were now. The inability to understand or hold space for compassion during this time created even more uneasiness and a greater lack of trust in the leadership.

Outcomes and Conclusion

At this time there has been no change other than negative impacts on retention. It is because of authority figures like this Chief that the Coast Guard and any other organization may struggle because the stressful environments that they create are a feeling of being unsafe in the workplace. I continue to advocate for those that are not feeling heard, seen, or safe at work due to this authority figure. We cannot call her a leader as she does not lead; it is abundantly clear that people like this need a great deal of education and self-reflection to move out of their egos. When the concern is only on themselves, they cannot be a true productive or compassionate leader.

Reflection Journal

We recommend you keep a journal to reflect and write, using these questions to prompt your thinking.

1. Egocentric leaders think about themselves and how actions will impact them. They typically have little regard for how others will be affected. Have you worked with a leader who had an egocentric nature?
2. How would you compare the characteristics of egocentric and narcissistic leaders?
3. Some people believe in tough love – that they need to enforce tight controls and be hard on people to get the most from them. Tough love is different from being tough on people due to a lack of care or empathy. Do you see the Chief's response as indicative of tough love or a lack of care?

Basic Questions

1. What evidence of egocentric behavior was present?
2. What were the outcomes of egocentric leadership in this situation?

Advanced Questions

1. What was the climate of the organization?
2. Do you agree that the behavior was egocentric?
3. The oppressed follower presented a watch rotation option, which the leader rejected by saying, "suck it up; it's hard for everyone". Was this appropriate language based on the military setting?

Questions for Leaders

1. Do you agree with the statement that people don't quit jobs; they quit leaders?
2. Did the organizational culture support the toxic behaviors?
3. After being counseled for her actions, the egocentric leader returned to the organization and rebuked her subordinates, stating, "you do not have the right to feel uneasy around me". How would you have ensured that the leader did not take action against her subordinates?

Case 10.2

Testimonial

I was working for a sales firm when I first experienced a toxic leader. This toxic leader created a culture of greed and was a hypocrite.

At first, sales were great and everyone on the team was making honest money. Then the Great Recession of 2008 happened. Before the Great Recession, our team leader was living large. He had just purchased a new car and large house in one of the nicest neighborhoods in the city. But after the financial collapse, sales dropped dramatically. In order to keep up the large lifestyle he had been accustomed to before the recession, our team leader had us lie on applications in order to inflate our sales. We were also told to lie to customers about specific terms of the application, in order to get them to close on the deals. If you supported this behavior and joined in, our team leader treated you as a favorite and that translated into additional benefits and bonuses. It seemed great, everyone making money, leadership was taking time off for expensive vacations, and we had many catered lunches. There was no doubt that greed and lust for money was what was driving the ship.

Environment

Our leader had many opportunities to do the right thing to help the entire department but instead would choose the path that benefited himself and his bonuses. The accountability within the organization was discouraging. While we were all making money, we knew what we were doing was wrong. Several of my colleagues spoke out against this environment of greed, and they were all fired within a week's time.

Outcome and Coping

After a few months I could no longer go on. The guilt and shame of what we were doing was not worth the money I was making. As an employee, I felt I had three options to cope. One, go along with the environment of greed and continue with the unethical practices. Two, speak out and get fired. And three, leave on my own. I chose the third option. A few months after I left, I found out that the department had been investigated and lawsuits were being filed against the firm. The team leader denied all knowledge of what had been going on. Come to find out, while he made us lie on applications and lie to customers, he never did it himself, even though he said he did all the time. This allowed him to look squeaky clean when everyone else got caught.

Reflection Journal

We recommend you keep a journal to reflect and write, using these questions to prompt your thinking.

1. The story speaks of an organizational culture of greed and excess. The oppressed follower reported feeling shame and guilt for participating in the unethical schemes. People who spoke out were fired. What were the primary polarities in this situation?
2. If a supervisor encourages or demands it, is it acceptable to bend or break a rule? Are there exceptions?

Basic Questions

1. What elements of the leader's behavior point to egocentric leadership?
2. What coping options did the oppressed follower identify?
3. What were the outcomes of the situation?

Advanced Questions

1. What were some of the elements of organizational culture?
2. What were the advantages of being in the in-group?
3. What were the disadvantages of being in the out-group?
4. What were other coping options besides the three mentioned by the oppressed follower?

Questions for Leaders

1. The oppressed follower reported that the team leader demanded that employees lie to customers and falsify the applications. Was this behavior justified?
2. Should firms have controls in place to prevent the falsification of applications?

3. Employees who did not go along with the scheme were fired. Was an effective offboarding process in place?
4. Does your organization conduct exit interviews to gather feedback from employees who resign or are terminated?
5. The team leader did not falsify applications or directly lie to customers, which "allowed him to look squeaky clean when everyone else got caught." Since he also denied knowing anything about the misconduct, should the organization retain him?

Case 10.3

Testimonial

I have had extensive experience with egocentric leaders; military organizations attract and retain type A personalities (for a very good reason), but egocentrism is an unwanted side effect to this desirable population base. The military career promotion structure unintentionally rewards egocentric personnel. For example, while climbing the ranks, I encountered many leaders who claimed my efforts and ideas as their own (and I may have subconsciously done the same). Leaders and managers are responsible for the team, which gives an egocentric leader justification for claiming recognition for the team's achievements. Another characteristic of egocentrism is the practice of favoritism. When you are 'in the crowd' of the leader's favorites, you are ranked higher and promoted without merit. This leads to a structure where top personnel lack competence, further undermining a culture of toxicity within an organization.

Environment Created

An egocentric leader promotes an environment of defensiveness, division, exclusion, and lack of follower development. When the leader takes credit for the accomplishment of the team for selfish gain, the followers feel used as a means to end. More specifically, followers are faced with the reality that they are just another tool used for the leader's status gain and continued climb up the ranks. Rather than a concerted effort toward a shared goal, the team is disharmonized into different and conflicting goals, namely, who gets the credit and how you can prove it. This type of proving personal success wastes organizational resources.

With favoritism, the organizational environment becomes one in which the group behaves to please the boss. Instead of voicing important disagreements, personnel just repeat what the leader wants to hear so that they are considered in the 'in-crowd'. Instead, the path toward a balanced and successful organization lies within the disagreement and dialogue that follows.

Favoritism also stunts the growth of employees who seek to progress without merit. It's the struggle where transformation and personal mastery occur; the grit to persevere through the process of true development. Pretending to be like the type of person the leader favors only hurts themselves.

Coping

Sadly, I haven't always coped with these environments like a saintly follower, but there have been times when I chose the noble path. It is very difficult to go against the grain in these environments. I specifically remember a time when a major military catastrophe occurred and my dive team was called in the middle of the night to respond. We slogged through roughly 3 weeks of effort in arduous conditions with little sleep or basic comfort. After the work was done certain individuals immediately began claiming supreme recognition for the work we accomplished, even to this day. I remember just keeping it to myself, thinking "hey, if they are willing to seek recognition, they must need it". After all, our promotions were on track anyway. During times when leaders were surrounded by favorites, I remember coping very poorly with this. I was either one of the favorites, or I was aligned with the group of misfits (which we proudly identified with).

End Results

During the times I was a favorite, my development as a leader came to a screeching halt. I didn't have to complete the difficult tasks that came along with the natural struggle of personal development – instead, shortcuts were taken because of my commitment to the leader's preference, and I didn't gain the lessons that would have been learned the right way. During the times when I didn't meet the in-crowd entry requirements, I remember seeking avoidance activities with my time during the day. The realization that hard work didn't mean promotion became salient and affected our behavior. Looking back, the entire organization suffered for the behaviors of toxic leaders. Time continued but the damage was done. Many learning opportunities were missed, attitudes shaped, and decisions made that can't be taken back.

Reflection Journal

We recommend you keep a journal to reflect and write, using these questions to prompt your thinking.

1. The writer stated that military organizations attract and retain Type A personalities and that egocentrism is an unwanted side effect. Do you agree with this characterization?
2. Many organizations rely on high-performing teams to meet their operational needs. At the same time, many of those organizations develop administrative systems that reward competition. These two values create a polarity between acting for the collective and acting in one's self-interest. The testimonial displays this dynamic in describing what it takes for high-performing team members to climb the military promotion ranks. What are the implications for leaders who must choose how to claim recognition for the team's achievements?
3. How do you make sense of the oppressed follower's claim that seeking credit for operational successes wastes organizational resources?

Basic Questions

1. What does the writer point to as evidence of egocentric leadership?
2. What does the oppressed follower see as the outcomes of egocentric leadership?
3. Did the oppressed follower exhibit effective coping strategies?

Advanced Questions

1. What were the effects of in-group and out-group membership?
2. The author argued that favoritism "stunts the growth of employees who seek to progress without merit". Conversely, members of the in-group often have access to extra resources and preferred developmental opportunities. How do you square these potentially conflicting perspectives?

Questions for Leaders

1. How should organizations structure reward and recognition systems for high-performing individuals and teams?
2. How can leaders ensure that in-group and out-group people have fair opportunities to participate in organizational rewards (e.g., promotion, compensation, developmental opportunities)?
3. What conditions are necessary to ensure that individuals at the lowest levels are empowered to demonstrate leadership and work toward mission accomplishment?

4. How can leaders avoid feelings of apathy and burnout so that they do not actively disengage from the organization?
5. Do you check in with your subordinate leaders to ensure that they are coping effectively with organizational stressors?

References

Han, G. H., Harms, P. D., & Bai, Y. (2017). Nightmare bosses: The impact of abusive supervision on employees' sleep, emotions, and creativity. *Journal of Business Ethics, 145*(1), 21–31. https://doi.org/10.1007/s10551-015-2859-y

Matos, K., O'Neill, O., & Lei, X. (2018). Toxic leadership and the masculinity contest culture: How "win or die" cultures breed abusive leadership. *Journal of Social Issues, 74*(3), 500–528. https://doi.org/10.1111/josi.12284

Rasool, G., Naseer, S., Syed, F., & Ahmed, I. (2018). Despotic leadership and employee's outcomes: Mediating effect of impression management. *Pakistan Journal of Commerce and Social Sciences, 12*(3), 784–806. https://go.exlibris.link/DQWnv3YH

Schaffer, H. R. (2006). *Key concepts in developmental psychology*. Sage.

Wegge, J., Shemla, M., & Haslam, S. A. (2014). Leader behavior as a determinant of health at work: Specification and evidence of five key pathways. *German Journal of Human Resource Management: Zeitschrift für Personalforschung, 28*(1–2), 6–23. https://doi.org/10.1177/239700221402800102

11 Emotional Dysregulation Cases

Emotional Dysregulation

Chapter 11 will discuss the category of *emotional dysregulation*. Emotional dysregulation (ED) is the inability of an individual to regulate emotions when compared with others of the same developmental level or age (Brancati et al., 2019). Individuals with ED suboptimally manage emotional intensity, direction, and duration. Researchers and clinicians also use other terms such as affective instability, mood instability, affective lability, and mood swings as synonymous with ED (Brancati et al., 2019; Marwaha et al., 2014). Affect refers to the outward expression of feelings and emotions, while lability means inconsistency.

Marwaha et al. (2014) conducted a metanalysis of ED literature. In some studies, researchers described ED as a trait and in others as a symptom. The differentiation is significant because several studies linked ED to attention-deficit and hyperactivity disorder (ADHD), borderline personality disorder (BLPD), and bipolar spectrum disorders (BPD). Thus, ED might be a symptom of ADHD, BLPD, or BPD, or it might be a personality trait.

There are three components of behavioral consequences: (1) oscillation of affect, (2) intensity of emotional responses, and (3) capacity to regulate emotional responses (Marwaha et al., 2014). Finally, it is not clear that changes in affect usually result from environmental cues. In other words, Marwaha et al. (2014) found that some studies pointed to environmental triggers while other studies did not point to such stimuli.

According to Gabriel (2016), toxic leaders lack emotional intelligence. Their inability to demonstrate empathy or regulate their emotions results in workplace environments riddled with fear and high turnover. Friedman and Gerstein (2017) echoed this conclusion, stating that millennials are especially allergic to emotionless leadership.

The following testimonials highlight aspects of emotional dysregulation.

DOI: 10.4324/9781003202462-11

Case 11.1

The Testimonial

My first experience with a toxic leader was with my high school basketball coach. We will call him Rob. Coach Rob was our school's chemistry teacher, and he was also the varsity basketball coach. Every day during the school year, we would have 6th-period basketball practice. During basketball season, we would have 6th-period basketball followed by our actual basketball practices (which would often take us to 7:00–8:00 pm at night). As an adult looking back, it is easy to understand why Coach Rob behaved the way that he did with us. Dealing with high school kids all day long is not an easy task. Nonetheless, Coach Rob did contribute to my first toxic leadership experience.

Environment

Every day at practice, he would bring all of his negative emotions from the day with him. The emotion he brought most often was anger. He often showed frustration, annoyance, irritability, and even fury towards us. Little did I know that each time he displayed these emotions towards us, it was influencing us in a negative way. Negative emotions are contagious. Since we were surrounded by anger and frustration every day, it tended to rub off on us. I would find myself leaving practice angry and always in a bad mood. Coach Rob was a good guy off of the court, but by not being able to regulate his negative emotions in practice with us, he ended up affecting a lot of our emotional states in the process.

Coping

Since my parents wouldn't allow me to quit the team, the only thing I could do was keep moving forward. Every day at practice, the team braced for another emotional outburst of anger from coach Rob, and every day we got it. Several of our best players ended up quitting the team. Those of us who did not have that luxury were trapped in an environment of fear. We were all happy when the season finally ended, and we no longer had to deal with coach Rob.

Reflection Journal

We recommend you keep a journal to reflect and write, using these questions to prompt your thinking.

1. Youth sports coaches have a tremendous developmental effect on their athletes. Should youth sports coaches focus on athletic performance over other developmental aspects such as character, resilience, and skills? In other words, is it all about the wins?
2. Individuals who work with children also exist outside of the classroom or off the field. How can teachers or coaches compartmentalize their private existence to prevent bringing their issues and challenges into their work?
3. As the colleague of an individual who might be exhibiting ED traits or symptoms, what steps would you need to take to intervene for your colleague or to protect the affected children?
4. Do you think older children benefit from being around adults like this coach? In other words, do kids need to be exposed to toxic individuals to get a taste of the real world?

Basic Questions

1. Does ED appear to be an issue in this situation?
2. What outcomes did the oppressed follower report?
3. What coping strategies did the followers use?

Advanced Questions

1. Do you think people who demonstrate ED symptoms are aware of their mood swings?
2. Do school systems have effective systems to prevent individual actors from exercising bad behavior?
3. What aspects of the school culture allowed the toxic behavior?

Questions for Leaders

1. Did the coach open the school to any potential liability in this situation?
2. As an educational leader, how would you handle this situation?
3. As a school administrator, what would you do if several student-athletes complained about their coach?
4. Does the school have a duty to inform parents of the situation?

Case 11.2

The Testimonial

In July of 2007, I had just finished my apprenticeship training in aircraft maintenance for the E-3 Airborne Warning & Control System (AWACS) as an Airman in the United States Air Force. I had been in the service a grand total of seven months before I found myself thrust onto the "flight line," as we colloquially referred to the area where all of the aircraft were parked when not flying and either preparing for their next flight or awaiting maintenance actions of some sort. Due to manning needs, I was scheduled to remain on the mid-shift working from 11:30 pm until 8:00 am each day. This is where I met my very first front-line supervisor that would soon become the person that I spent the next fifteen months dreading to see on a daily basis, and whom I vowed to never emulate when it became my time to lead Airman in the future. Essentially, this supervisor was, to me, everything that I did not want to be as a leader.

My supervisor was a very gruff person that was newly minted as a front-line supervisor and I was one of his first two subordinates. He knew his job well but could not effectively teach the many tasks it entailed. This supervisor had a short temper and would yell at or denigrate others if they did not understand or hear him. This happened quite frequently as his normal conversational tone was quite low in volume. Due to this, it was perceived that he was simply upset a majority of the time at work.

One night I had come to this supervisor in emotional distress; I was having a difficult time physically coping with the work schedule, my personal life was suffering because of it, and I expressed how much I disdained coming into work each night fearful for what possible disappointment I may generate in him. His reaction was utterly emotionless as he sat there listening to my concerns while I was on the verge of tears. Once I had aired my grievances, he told me that there was nothing he'd do for me, that the shift I was scheduled on was what I required and to essentially "suck it up". I never approached him again with my concerns after this encounter.

Environment

Every day, I would drive into work wondering what mood my supervisor would be in, or holding on to the hope that I'd be paired with another technician for the night for our maintenance tasks. My peers witnessed my slow descent into depression and shared an equal disdain for occasionally having to work with this supervisor. This constant fear clouded my understanding of my greater contribution and I did not fully understand my role in the Air Force. I knew that I came in every night and helped repair aircraft, but I had no idea what the impact of my actions enabled. The environment I operated in at the time allowed this supervisor to continue to haunt me, it was even mildly encouraged as it was thought that the best learning comes through "tough love".

Coping

To survive in this environment, I sought the validation of my concerns from my peers; I was too fearful to elevate my issues beyond that of my supervisor. For a while, my peers helped me through the tough times as an ear to listen to my difficulties; my wife was also helpful as I knew I could be entirely candid with her. Ultimately, however, the only way out of my situation presented itself in the form of a Permanent Change of Station (PCS). After being at this location for a year and a half, I had a golden ticket to move somewhere else, somewhere that I believed could not possibly be as bad as my current situation. I earned a change in my life, one that I felt was imperative for me continue. This was the only ultimate coping mechanism that would lift me from the waking nightmare.

Outcome

Through the experience of those tumultuous fifteen months, I grew. Unbeknownst to me at the time, I was learning valuable lessons in leadership before I had actually received any formal education or training in it. I learned that the positional power that a supervisor holds over a subordinate can affect their work performance but, more importantly, their mental state also. I learned various traits that I did not want to emulate; but most importantly, I developed emotional intelligence and a desire to pursue a Servant Leadership style. In the years to follow, I became a front-line supervisor, and eventually a middle-manager. I gained a wealth of knowledge on the processes that are in place to help prevent the situation I described above. I learned that what my supervisor did back in 2007 and 2008 was not "okay", and while I am not grateful to him for the experience, I am a better leader because of it.

Reflection Journal

We recommend you keep a journal to reflect and write, using these questions to prompt your thinking.

1. The oppressed follower described a journey from being brand new, to physical and emotional distress, to feeling trapped and isolated, and to ultimately developing the resilience to develop emotional intelligence and hone a servant leadership style.
2. Military systems promote people into supervisorial roles. There is no technical path where a service member can advance in rank yet remain in a purely technical capacity. What are the implications of this system?
3. Do you think that all people have a capacity to develop effective leadership and managerial skills?

Basic Questions

1. What behaviors did the oppressed follower describe?
2. Do the issues point toward emotional dysregulation?
3. What outcomes did the oppressed follower report?
4. What coping strategies did the followers use?

Advanced Questions

1. Was the oppressed follower's behavior enabling?
2. What other options might the follower have used to deal with the toxic supervisor?
3. What options might the collective group of followers have used to deal with the situation?

Questions for Leaders

1. How should newer employees be enculturated into an organization?
2. How does the answer change if the employees are also inexperienced in the workplace and new?
3. Do the onboarding processes in your organization focus on technical skills, or do they also cover cultural aspects of the organization?
4. What can managers do if a personality mismatch exists between a supervisor and a worker?
5. How might you have handled the situation in which your subordinate confided feelings of emotional and physical distress due to workplace conditions?
6. What sort of training would be most helpful for the toxic supervisor?

Case 11.3

The Testimonial

I have experienced my share of toxic leadership in my time. The period that stands out for me the most are my first 7 years working in education. I was thrilled when I landed my job at the college. I honestly thought this was going to be my dream job, but my big dreams of the perfect job came crashing down shortly after I started when I realized that the environment was cruel, never changing, and all due to one toxic individual and a director's inability to do right by all of us and lead. To say that this reality was heartbreaking really doesn't cover it.

This leader had a complete inability to regulate her emotions. She hoarded information to make herself indispensable and we were not allowed to make mistakes without being blasted with anger, criticism, and embarrassment. We fixed errors, covered them up, and hoped that she would never find them. There was humiliation and shaming, and it was extremely belittling. There was never compassion or trust. None of us ever felt that this leader had our best interest at heart. She was always on edge and on the verge of an emotional outburst aimed at anyone and everyone. Questioning methods or the status quo was never welcome, and retaliation was a norm.

Environment

This was not a learning, creative, or innovating environment. This was a tense, cover-you-behind, watch your back, speak when spoken to, deflating environment. We were not empowered or inspired, and as the new girl, I very much felt like the scapegoat for any backlash.

Coping

At first, I coped with this environment defensively. I came into this environment confident and eager. I was eager to learn and bring my knowledge and experience to light but that was not welcomed. I found myself constantly defending myself. Leaving was not an option. I was the primary source of income for my family and the country had entered a recession because of the financial crisis. This meant jobs were scarce and the college was on a hiring freeze. Over time, I became timid and defeated. I had no confidence, started to blame myself, and started to think that I was the problem. Once positions started to open around the college, I started to apply but lacked confidence in my abilities. The outreach work and connections I made outside of the office helped, and my allies started looking out for me. When I was finally offered another position, it was a lateral move but an opportunity nonetheless. I was pregnant at the time and ready to have my second child in a matter of weeks, so the self-doubt was even more unbearable. A wonderful friend talked me into taking the position and my new manager didn't care that I was going to be out on maternity leave soon, she just wanted me as part of her team. That manager and I are still friends now. Finally, I was out and could start to work on myself again, but I was deeply afraid that I would go from bad to worse and wasn't sure how much more I could take. Luckily that was not the case.

Outcome

Once I left that toxic environment, someone else took my place and after a few months, my replacement reached out to me. They too were experiencing the same issues and wanted my feedback on how to best handle the environment and that toxic leader. "You were there for so long", she said, "what was your secret". My secret was, I did it for my family and we were in a recession. That individual moved on after six months and the next person also reached out – she left too. What can be learned from toxic environments? While I would never want to relive that experience or that environment, I am grateful for the lessons. I learned about the kind of person, colleague, leader, and human being I want to be both in my personal life and in my professional life. I learned compassion, kindness, strength, the ability to be tactful and assertive. Over time, I learned to have confidence again and how to step into my power and speak up in a way that is both empathetic and impactful. Yet, after all this time, I still find my imposter syndrome getting the best of me from time to time. Thankfully, I also learned how to embrace being a learner and being an imperfect work-in-progress, and that is ok.

Reflection Journal

We recommend you keep a journal to reflect and write, using these questions to prompt your thinking.

1. Learning organizations are characterized by high levels of trust and knowledge sharing. In 1991, the *Harvard Business Review* published an influential article by Ikujiro Nonaka titled "The Knowledge-Creating

Company". Nonaka (1991) argued that competitive advantage springs from creating new knowledge, disseminating it widely through a company, and working that knowledge into new products and services. The toxic manager in this story hoarded information from her employees and destroyed trust. What might cause a manager to hoard essential information from employees?
2. The oppressed follower remained in her job because of the economy and her lack of confidence to find a new position. Do you think that toxic leaders intentionally create dependent followers, effectively holding them hostage?
3. Stockholm syndrome is commonly used to describe positive emotional bonds that kidnaps victims develop toward their captors (Namnyak et al., 2008). Also referred to as terror bonding or traumatic bonding, Stockholm syndrome is not recognized as a psychiatric condition. Nevertheless, the literature describes four common features related to media accounts of Stockholm syndrome: the captor threatened the victim directly; the victim was isolated; the victim could have escaped but did not; and the victim sympathized with the captor, postcaptivity. Do you see any relationship between Stockholm syndrome and how oppressed followers represent survival of their toxic situations?

Basic Questions

1. Does ED appear to be an issue in this situation?
2. What coping strategies did the followers use?
3. What outcomes did the oppressed follower report?

Advanced Questions

1. Have you noticed similarities in how oppressed followers perceived organizational climate and toxic leadership characteristics?
2. How did the oppressed follower characterize interaction with the organization, other followers, and her family?
3. The oppressed follower stayed in the job for seven years. What issues did this create for her career and well-being?

Questions for Leaders

1. How would you describe the toxic manager's leadership style and philosophy?
2. The oppressed follower remained in the job for seven years and spoke of her successors who left after several months. This means that the toxic leader was in the same position for at least eight years. Is it common for mid-level managers to remain in the same position for eight years?

3. What are potential implications of such a lengthy tenure in terms of developmental opportunities, knowledge sharing, innovation, and human resource management?

References

Brancati, G. E., Barbuti, M., Pallucchini, A., Cotugno, B., Schiavi, E., Hantouche, E. G., & Perugi, G. (2019). Reactivity, intensity, polarity and stability questionnaire (ripost-40) assessing emotional dysregulation: Development, reliability and validity. *Journal of Affective Disorders*, *257*, 187–194. https://doi.org/10.1016/j.jad.2019.07.028

Friedman, H. H., & Gerstein, M. (2017). Leading with compassion: The key to changing the organizational culture and achieving success. *Psychosociological Issues in Human Resource Management*, *5*(1), 160–175. https://doi.org/10.22381/PIHRM5120175

Gabriel, J. M. O. (2016). Supervisors' toxicity as predictor of subordinates' counterproductive work behavior in Nigerian public hospitals. *Journal of Applied Business Research*, *32*(5), 1363. https://doi.org/10.19030/jabr.v32i5.9765

Marwaha, S., He, Z., Broome, M., Singh, S. P., Scott, J., Eyden, J., & Wolke, D. (2014). How is affective instability defined and measured? A systematic review. *Psychological Medicine*, *44*(9), 1793–1808. https://doi.org/10.1017/S0033291713002407

Namnyak, M., Tufton, N., Szekely, R., Toal, M., Worboys, S., & Sampson, E. L. (2008). Stockholm syndrome: Psychiatric diagnosis or urban myth? *Acta Psychiatrica Scandinavica*, *117*(1), 4–11. https://doi.org/10.1111/j.1600-0447.2007.01112.x

Nonaka, I. (1991). The knowledge-creating company. *Harvard Business Review*, *69*(6), 96.

12 Ineffective Leadership Cases

Ineffective Leadership

Chapter 12 will discuss the category of *ineffective leadership*. Even the best leaders are ineffective at times. We describe ineffective leadership as habitual leadership patterns or styles that cause followers to lose trust in their leaders' abilities to meet organizational objectives. In a study conducted by Paltu and Brouwers (2020), leadership that consisted of micromanaging, blaming, and setting unrealistic goals led to organizational toxicity. These toxic behaviors resulted in toxic organizational cultures where employees were less committed to the organization, leading to high turnover rates and low levels of job satisfaction and productivity. In similar studies, Dobbs (2014) and Schmidt (2014) found that ineffective and unreliable leadership resulted in deleterious effects on the overall organization and its outcomes.

The following testimonials highlight aspects of ineffective leadership.

Case 12.1

The Testimonial

My current supervisor most closely resembles the ineffective toxic leadership typology. She uses behaviors that are not conducive to a healthy working environment such as having unrealistic expectations of her subordinates, constantly placing blame onto others when things go wrong, and micromanaging tasks. She adds unrealistic deadlines to her subordinates as well as contacting us when we are using paid time off for the day; there is no legitimate work life balance as a result of her behaviors. She is also very quick to point the finger onto her subordinates when something unfavorable occurs and will not take any responsibility for her contributions to the event. Over the last two months, she has specifically utilized the public humiliation behavior with me in front of my colleagues, which is a true testament to her

DOI: 10.4324/9781003202462-12

toxic style of leadership. When I had a conversation with her about these unappreciated events, it became quite evident she lacked emotional intelligence and self-awareness and stated that I was the one that was misunderstood and that my complaints had no merits. I then provided her with examples of what she said on the calls that proved she had been ridiculing me in front of others, and she quickly brushed her comments aside and said I needed to grow up. Her lack of ability to reflect on her actions was wildly alarming to me. It was at this moment that I realized she does not listen to any feedback from her subordinates, and that is dangerous for an organization. These toxic behaviors are directly responsible for creating a hostile and unpleasant working environment.

Environment

My supervisor's ineffective leadership is directly responsible for creating a toxic organizational culture within our region. As a result, the directors do not wish to collaborate with her and are afraid to speak up out of fear of retaliation. It goes without saying that the morale is low among our team, and we feel like we are constantly walking on eggshells because we never know what we are going to get from her each day. When I first started with the organization, unbeknownst to me, she needed to fill three out of seven director positions due to unfavorable turnover. I specifically remember in my interview with her that she spoke of low director turnover rates. After I was hired, I quickly realized that was not the case and was immediately concerned. Additionally, I quickly learned that she was in litigation with at least two of her former directors for complaints of psychological warfare and creating a hostile working environment. The environment has not improved and has become increasingly worse over the last couple of months, which have made it extremely difficult to cope with.

Outcome and Coping

I am a firm believer that effective communication is one of the most frequently seen deficits with leaders and my supervisor is no exception. As her behaviors worsened with me over the last few months, I knew I needed to approach her and have a productive conversation with her. My first conversation with her mid-March went surprisingly. I left the conversation feeling hopeful that things would improve moving forward and that she understood her need to improve her communications. Unfortunately, less than two weeks after that conversation, she and I had the worst interaction we had ever had. She called me over concerns with two patient charts and proceeded to yell, belittle me, and tell me she would not help me to correct the issue because I "should know better by now". This interaction left me in tears, and I felt defeated yet angry that I was being subjected to this type of psychological torture. I called her the next day to explain my corrective action for the patient charts, and to my surprise, she was pleasant on the phone and even cracked jokes and laughed. I made excuses for her and told myself she must have had a bad day yesterday and I took everything too personal. Less than a week later, she began to publicly humiliate me on our leadership calls, and I again found myself in tears and feeling shame and defeat. I had more subsequent conversations with her about her ineffective leadership and finally said, "I cannot continue like this. I do not have an issue with feedback, but I do have concerns with your approach and quite frankly, you are creating a hostile working environment and I need that to change." When things did not improve, I packed up my personal belongings in my office on a particularly rough day and knew I needed to look for employment elsewhere. My coping mechanisms had run out, and I no longer cared about giving my all for a supervisor I did not respect. The outcome resulted in me giving my notice earlier this week.

Toxic leadership is costly for an organization and results in litigations, low morale, uncommitted employees, and high turnover. My supervisor created an environment that was hostile, non-collaborative, and fearful in nature and my coping mechanisms resulted in me resigning and looking for an employer who is not toxic. While my supervisor is undoubtedly one of the worst I've ever experienced, I have learned exactly how I do not want to be in my future leadership roles. My hope for all organizations is that they understand the impact that ineffective leadership can have on their team and make every effort to hire inspirational and effective leaders.

Reflection Journal

We recommend you keep a journal to reflect and write, using these questions to prompt your thinking.

1. How would you react if you were on a phone call with several colleagues and heard a supervisor publicly berating or attacking an employee?
2. Do you think that people are too thin-skinned? In other words, do most people not take criticism well?
3. How do you react to criticism that you believe is unjustified? What about criticism that you think is justified?
4. What do you think about the claim that the toxic leader misrepresented the turnover in her group during the interview process?

Basic Questions

1. What ineffective leader characteristics did the follower observe?
2. What were the outcomes of the toxic leader's actions?
3. What coping mechanisms did the oppressed follower use?

Advanced Questions

1. In addition to ineffective leadership, do you detect signs of emotional dysregulation?
2. If no one speaks up or stops public attacks, what impact does that have on the organizational climate?
3. What sort of organizational culture would allow an atmosphere of public humiliation?

Questions for Leaders

1. What sort of training or other intervention would you recommend for the toxic supervisor?
2. The oppressed follower noted that the supervisor was involved in litigation with two former directors. How would you handle this situation from the perspective of the supervisor's manager?
3. How would you handle complaints that one of your employees created a hostile work environment?
4. Would your answer change based on the organizational level of the individual?
5. After the oppressed follower confronted the toxic supervisor, should the follower have also notified human resources or higher-level managers of the issue?
6. What organizational systems should protect employees from ineffective leaders?

Case 12.2

The Testimonial

The toxic leader I experienced spent most of her time micromanaging her employees and finding who to blame for assignments that she did not complete in order to hand off the responsibility to someone else. She spent most of her time avoiding responsibility and creating frustration for her team members. It was very difficult to have a conversation with her because she changed her mind so often that it was impossible to keep track of her thoughts. She rarely provided a definitive answer and avoided arriving at conclusions by shifting the conversation to discuss how bad of an employee you were and how she thought you could improve. There was an internal joke among her team members about who she was "out to get" this time because it felt like she was on a schedule to micromanage her team. Although this was not really funny because her behavior had serious repercussions for the department, it was a way for us to cope with her leadership style.

Environment

I worked under her for a total of four years and throughout that time, I witnessed several employees leave and was involved in formal complaints from other employees. As a matter of fact, a few months after I started employment, I was called to Human Resources for an ongoing investigation regarding her behavior. I realized early on that she would not be the easiest person to work with, let alone be part of her team. Most of her subordinates had worked with her for some time and knew what that entailed; therefore, our team meetings were unproductive and guided by complaints. She set unrealistic goals for us knowing that they would not be accomplished and had condescending responses to employees when they attempted to rationalize with her. Her behavior was communicated to her supervisors, but from what we encountered, nothing changed. The most unfair event that I witnessed was a coworker that was placed on administrative leave for a problem that she had with our supervisor and never came back to work. I found out later that she resigned from her position because she was being held accountable for something that was not her responsibility. This created a work culture where most of her followers were uncommitted to her goals and vision for the department.

Outcome and Coping

I personally coped with my supervisor's leadership style by working harder. I took on responsibilities that were not mine because I did not want to see our team fail. I believe that because of this, she rarely micromanaged me. The only issue I had with her occurred during an interaction with her supervisor where she lied about the direction she had given her team to avoid responsibility. Of course, there is also the mental exhaustion that I went through and the hostile environment that she created. Other members of the team coped with her behavior differently. As previously mentioned, there were a few employees that filed formal complaints against her. In addition, interdepartmental whistleblowing occurred a couple of times, and of course there was the employee that resigned from her position, which could be categorized as submission. Most importantly, her leadership style created low morale, discouragement, employee turnover, increased stress, and overall low efficiency.

The outcome of my story is that I looked for another job that ended in a promotion. Unfortunately, I cannot say the same for other members of the team. When I left, they had just hired an employee to replace the coworker that resigned, but it did not go well for her either. She kept in touch with me as I was the one training her before I left, and it was very sad to hear that she also filed a complaint and eventually resigned from her position as well. This is a perfect example of what toxic leadership does to organizations and how it negatively impacts operations and employee morale. I hope that something is done about her behavior, otherwise things might never change for the department.

Reflection Journal

We recommend you keep a journal to reflect and write, using these questions to prompt your thinking.

1. Many of the stories we collected shared a theme of the toxic leader blaming subordinates for operational failures. Do you think this behavior is only possible when organizational cultures encourage or support leaders in shifting blame to others?
2. A stretch goal is an "organizational goal with an objective probability of attainment that may be unknown but is seemingly impossible" given current practices, skills, and knowledge (Sitkin et al., 2011, p. 547). Some researchers argue that stretch goals disrupt complacency and promote innovation and action (Sitkin et al., 2011). Oppressed followers sometimes note that their supervisors set impossible goals, reducing trust and creating apathy. How does one balance the polarity between *stretch goals* and *achievable goals* without alienating subordinates?
3. Intelligent risks are risks in which the potential benefit outweighs the threat (Watkins & Denney, 2020). Learning organizations encourage intelligent risk-taking and see mistakes as learning opportunities. How

would the toxic environment described in the story affect organizational learning, innovation, and intelligent risk-taking?

Basic Questions

1. What ineffective leadership behaviors did the toxic leader display?
2. What organizational outcomes resulted from the toxic leader's behavior?
3. How did the followers cope with the toxic leader?

Advanced Questions

1. In your opinion, was the follower who wrote this story an oppressed follower, an ally to oppressed followers, or a conspirator of the toxic leader?
2. Were power and influence balanced toward the leaders or the followers?
3. The team members in this story bonded over discussing the issues with the toxic leader. What coping actions might they have taken collectively to deal with the toxic leader?

Questions for Leaders

1. Why do you think the toxic leader survived multiple complaints to supervisors and human resources?
2. In your organization, what level of ineffectiveness would cause human resources to sanction a supervisor?
3. Are the odds stacked against employees who report toxic leaders?
4. What could organizations do to make the system more effective from the subordinate's perspective?
5. Many departments suffer from high levels of turnover. This can be a sign of leadership problems. Does your organization monitor and attempt to diagnose the reasons for high turnover?

Case 12.3

The Testimonial

My supervisor had a reputation for being a successful businesswoman in the small border town of El Centro, California. Her employees and volunteers had the misfortune of seeing the reality of her ineffective leadership.

In 2014, I was fresh out of high school and passionate about my love for animals. I would volunteer at the animal shelter, my local veterinarian, and a horse ranch that provided therapy for special needs children and adults; you name it, I was there. My weekends were dedicated to gaining experience in the animal care field. Naturally, I applied to be a volunteer at the brand-new canine boarding center. It was a luxury in my small hometown of El Centro, CA. I was ecstatic at the opportunity to volunteer at a facility that had modern kennels, top-tier brand food, and an outside turf area for the dogs. My heart just about leaped out of my chest the moment I got the news I was accepted.

My first couple of days were spent learning how to function as a part of the team. The idea of a happy work environment and team dynamic felt exciting for me; I came to find out it was an illusion created by my toxic supervisor. I was tasked with cleaning, bookkeeping, customer service, and, my favorite, caring for the dogs. I was flushed with excitement at the fact that they trusted me, a 17-year-old, with caring for over 20 dogs. I felt proud of myself for earning my supervisors' trust in just the span of a few days. I was not like any other volunteer or employee. Some take pride in arts and crafts, exercising, and writing; I take pride in putting in my best effort at work, even if it is menial.

Week after week, I would clock in, perform my tasks with a smile on my face, and go home to look forward to the next day of work. Then, my coworkers started to get paid for their work, although they had volunteer positions just like me. I couldn't help but feel jealous and insecure. Why haven't they started paying me? Is my work not good enough? Do they not like me as a person? Nevertheless, I kept my head down and continued to do my best.

One day, my supervisor requested that I come in at 5:00 am. I was merely 5 minutes late, which had never happened before. I apologized for my tardiness and explained it would never happen again. My supervisor seemed to understand and went about her business. However, later that day, she pulled me into her office to talk to me. She told me that the co-owner had advised her to fire me for being late and that she did not agree but is hesitant about trusting me now. Upon hearing her say that, I immediately broke into tears. My coworkers make mistakes all the time and never get spoken to like this. Still, I kept my head down and continued to do my best.

Throughout my time as a volunteer, I nurtured a healthy working relationship with my coworkers. It seemed the more my coworkers and I laughed and spoke, the more productive we were, the less our supervisor smiled at us. Day after day, my supervisor started adding new rules. First, she told us, "It would be best if you didn't talk during your shift." She continued to add task after task to the point where it became impossible to complete everything she assigned. She made a point to add cameras at the facility to micromanage us and make sure we were working and not speaking to one another. It made me feel uncomfortable, but I was not doing anything wrong, so I convinced myself it would be fine to be monitored during my shifts.

I began to feel anxious going to volunteer, and my supervisor noticed. But she offered me the paid job I was waiting for this entire time. I excitedly accepted, already feeling better, thinking that my supervisor appreciated my work. Yet, she continued to become stricter. She would call us on the phone, letting us know she was watching, and she saw us talking while we were mopping and sweeping. While we played with the dogs outside, she wanted us on opposite ends of the field. She went on to not schedule us for shifts together anymore.

My last day working for my supervisor was the worst experience I've had with a superior. I reached out to the groomer that was contracted by my supervisor to get services for my dog. The groomer did not respond, which I found strange. The next day, my supervisor told me I was being disloyal to her because she had expressed concerns about the groomer to me confidentially a few days ago. Although this was not my topic of conversation with the groomer, she assumed I was gossiping. As a 17-year-old being treated this way by a successful 40-year-old woman, I could not help but feel shame and embarrassment, thinking it was my fault for reaching out to the groomer. I went home that day and cried to my mother, who gave me a lesson on self-worth. I could not face another moment working for a supervisor that was making me question my value as a person. I never went back after that. My coworkers quickly began to leave the business after that.

Environment

First, the supervisor displayed characteristics of an ineffective leader through her use of nepotism, setting unrealistic goals, micromanaging, and inability to communicate. Her relationship with her subordinates, in my perspective, suffered due to a lack of communication about the promotions she was offering some employees. She created a culture of insecurity and jealousy in her employees. Instead of creating a hostile environment, she could have had a simple dialogue to celebrate the promotions of these employees as a team and make the requirements for promotion available.

Second, another ineffective leadership characteristic my supervisor displayed was that she was open about the gossip that was happening about the employees. When she discussed me being late, she mentioned that her business partner would like to see me fired over a minor and genuine mistake. She made the comment personal to me because she told me she did not trust me. This happened again when I approached the contracted groomer. It was clear she saw me as a machine and not a human. She was creating a false sense of trust and loyalty. A great leader would instead see the humanity in the employee and, only if it becomes a pattern, provide corrective action that provides a solution. An effective leader would also not create a divide between her staff and contractors but bring them together.

Last, her unrealistic expectations set on me and the other employees were another ineffective leader trait she practiced. She assigned her staff an unreasonable number of tasks, and when we did not have time to complete the list, she became disgruntled with us. My supervisor wanted to maintain her superiority within the team and kept adding to the list until she could state we did not perform the full duties of our jobs. Instead, she could have given us an appropriate amount of time to complete each task with reasonable expectations.

Outcome

My former supervisor was a textbook example of an ineffective leader and gave me a clear picture of the leader I never want to become. As a manager now, I aim to continue building a healthy work environment for all staff and volunteers, where they have transparency, open dialogue, and a strong leader they trust to help them problem-solve. I will never gossip about my employees or volunteers, make them feel subpar, or create unrealistic expectations for them. Although it was a traumatizing coming-of-age experience, I am grateful for the learning lesson that has helped me practice strong leadership skills.

Reflection Journal

We recommend you keep a journal to reflect and write, using these questions to prompt your thinking.

1. Organizations that use long-term volunteers must take steps to motivate them to stay on the job (Millette & Gagné, 2008). Hackman and Oldham (as cited in Millette & Gagné, 2008) identified critical factors (i.e., job characteristics) to improve autonomous motivation, satisfaction, and performance.
    a. skill variety, the degree to which a job requires a variety of activities in carrying out the work;
    b. task identity, the degree to which a job requires completion of a whole and identifiable piece of work;

   c. task significance, the degree to which the job has a substantial impact on the lives of other people;
   d. autonomy, the degree to which the job provides substantial freedom, independence, and discretion; and
   e. feedback from the job, the degree to which carrying out the work activities provides direct and clear information about performance effectiveness. (Millette & Gagné, 2008, p. 12)

Did the toxic leader violate any of these motivational factors?

2. The oppressed follower described arriving five minutes late for a 5:00 a.m. shift. The supervisor later counseled the follower for arriving late. Were the supervisor's expectations reasonable, given the shift's start time change?

Basic Questions

1. What ineffective leader characteristics did the follower describe?
2. What coping mechanisms did the oppressed follower use?
3. What were the outcomes of the toxic leader's actions?

Advanced Questions

1. Would a more experienced volunteer have coped differently with the situation?
2. How did the toxic leader affect the oppressed follower's engagement and commitment to the organization?
3. Did the toxic leader prevent the followers from being effective in their roles?

Questions for Leaders

1. Do volunteers need to be treated differently than paid workers?
2. Was it reasonable to demand that the workers not interact during their shifts?
3. How would you react if you discovered your business partner was an ineffective leader?

References

Dobbs, J. M. (2014). *The relationship between perceived toxic leadership styles, leader effectiveness, and organizational cynicism* [Dissertation]. ProQuest Dissertations Publishing. https://go.exlibris.link/zr5KvJKs

Millette, V., & Gagné, M. (2008). Designing volunteers' tasks to maximize motivation, satisfaction and performance: The impact of job characteristics on volunteer engagement. *Motivation and Emotion*, *32*(1), 11–22. https://doi.org/10.1007/s11031-007-9079-4

Paltu, A., & Brouwers, M. (2020). Toxic leadership: Effects on job satisfaction, commitment, turnover intention and organisational culture within the South African manufacturing industry. *SA Journal of Human Resource Management*, *18*(1), 1–11. https://doi.org/10.4102/sajhrm.v18i0.1338

Schmidt, A. A. (2014). *An examination of toxic leadership, job outcomes, and the impact of military deployment* [Dissertation, University of Maryland]. ProQuest Dissertations Publishing.

Sitkin, S. B., See, K. E., Miller, C. C., Lawless, M. W., & Carton, A. M. (2011). The paradox of stretch goals: Organizations in pursuit of the seemingly impossible. *The Academy of Management Review*, *36*(3), 544–566. https://doi.org/10.5465/AMR.2011.61031811

Watkins, D. V., & Denney, V. P. (2020). The intelligent risk equation: When opportunities outweigh threats. *The Chronicle of Leadership and Management*, *1*(1), 37–54. https://baldrigefoundation.org/what-we-do/thought-leadership/clm/access-the-clm/

13 Moral Corruption Cases

Moral Corruption

Chapter 13 will discuss the category of *moral corruption*. Morally corrupt leaders do not care for the well-being of their followers (De Clercq et al., 2021). Cote (2018) contended that darker leadership styles resulted from moral-less and unethical leadership. For Cote, unethical leader behaviors included lying, bullying, corruption, and coercion to influence followers. Belal et al. (2021) argued that despotic leadership is the worst form of negative leadership because the leaders manipulate followers through moral corruption and information distortion. Additionally, such leadership is highly self-centered, vengeful, exploitative, authoritarian, and self-interested.

Morally corrupt leaders are responsible for effects such as diminished trust, engagement (Riffut & Nazahah, 2020), creativity, organizational citizenship, job performance, psychological well-being, and work–life balance (Belal et al., 2021; Shazia et al., 2020). Morally corrupt leaders created organizational climates that hindered creativity and productivity and lowered morale (Cote, 2018; Riffut & Nazahah, 2020). Morally corrupt leadership correlates with turnover, emotional exhaustion, downstream bullying, and conspiracy (Belal et al., 2021). The adverse outcomes are not limited to the workplace; the effects extend to families, customers, and society (Riffut & Nazahah, 2020).

One study found that followers can mitigate some effects of morally corrupt leaders through upward ingratiating behaviors such as exercising political behaviors, complimenting leaders, or emphasizing their accomplishments (De Clercq et al., 2021). Furthermore, according to Zhou et al. (2021), employees are more likely to expose leaders or quit because of access to information and corresponding cultural empowerment.

The following testimonials highlight aspects of moral corruption.

DOI: 10.4324/9781003202462-13

Case 13.1

The Testimonial

It was 2006, and I had just graduated with my bachelor's in business administration. I got my first job out of school at a corporate bank as a loan officer. The pay and benefits packages were good, and it initially felt like a great fit for a first job out of college. In 2006 the real estate market was booming. Everyone was buying, flipping, and investing in property.

A few months after I started, things changed. Our branch leader called me intc his office on a Friday afternoon and asked me if I wanted to make more money every month. "Of course", I said.

"Well, good. That's what I wanted to hear. But I'm going to need you to bend the rules a bit." He said.

"How so?" I asked.

"For starters, start telling clients you have a master's in finance. This will make them trust you more."

"OK . . . but I don't. I only have a bachelor's in business." I responded.

"That's OK!" he said firmly. "I don't care! I won't say anything, and no one will know."

Before I had time to respond, he started to discuss the second "change" he needed from me. "Secondly", he began, "we need to push more home loans through every month, so I'm gonna need you to fudge some numbers on client applications. Make sure their earnings are enough to cover their loan."

"So, you want me to lie on an application?" I asked.

He looked at me and smiled. "No one will know. It isn't a big deal. Don't overthink it."

He ushered me out of his office and wished me a good weekend.

Impact on the Organizational Environment

That weekend I couldn't get the conversation with my boss out of my head. I felt physically sick. What he was asking me to do was not only lying but illegal. I was young and didn't want to upset my boss at my very first "good" job out of college, but I also didn't want to break the law.

The next week I went into the office, and I kept my head down and tried not to be noticed. As loan applications came in,

I couldn't get myself to lie and fudge the numbers like my boss had told me to.

I dreaded going into work every day. I knew that if I did not listen to my boss and do what he said, there would eventually be another conversation between the two of us.

Coping

I coped by not obeying his orders to lie on applications. I started to get more stressed and felt physically sick that I would eventually get in trouble for not doing what my leader expected. I was depressed because this was my first good job, and I did not want to look like a failure by getting fired. I felt trapped.

Outcome

After a few weeks of me declining applications for unqualified individuals, my boss called me into his office. I knew this was it. He was going to ask me why I wasn't pushing more applications through.

"You know why I called you in here?" he was angry.

I stayed quiet.

"I thought you and I had an understanding? What is going on? Do you not have what it takes? Don't you want to make money?! I need you to be a team player!"

"I can't get myself to lie and do something illegal," I finally responded.

"No one is going to know!" He yelled. "You know what? Maybe you don't have what it takes. When I hired you, I thought you were a team player. I guess I was wrong."

I didn't know what to say.

"I am giving you one more chance. Now get out of my office." He slammed the door behind me.

The next week I quit. I was only there for six months, but the illegal activity that was expected of me was not worth the money and benefits.

In September of 2008, the real estate and financial markets collapsed. The corporate bank I had worked for went bankrupt and shut down three months later.

Reflection Journal

We recommend you keep a journal to reflect and write, using these questions to prompt your thinking.

1. Greed was rampant in the early 2000s, partially leading to the subprime market bubble burst (Avramenko & Boyd, 2013; Jones & Sirmans,

2019). Avramenko and Boyd (2013) suggested that "public policy can be an important tool in fostering what we call the 'subprime virtues' of truth-telling, promise-keeping, frugality, moderation, commitment, foresight, and judgment that are absolute prerequisites for any decent society" (p. 111). The toxic leader in this story eschewed these so-called subprime virtues, instead favoring to cash in on the market frenzy. Is greed such a powerful motivator that we must rely on public policy to foster virtuous behavior?

2. Bertland (2009) argued that organizational cultures that do not allow employees to question managers and promote competing ideas are corrupt. Bertland's argument derived from the capabilities approach to virtue ethics pioneered by Amartya Sen and extended by Martha Nussbaum. They believed that organizations "must provide opportunities for individuals to develop capabilities to function at a level worthy of human dignity" (Bertland, 2009, p. 25). Did this organizational culture appear to elevate human capabilities in such a way as to promote human dignity?

Basic Questions

1. What unethical behaviors did the toxic leader demand from the oppressed follower?
2. What did the toxic leader do that was unethical?
3. What climate did the toxic leader create when the oppressed follower refused to follow his demands?

Advanced Questions

1. Did the organizational culture seem to support the toxic leader?
2. Would the oppressed follower have been justified in following the toxic leader's orders?
3. If the toxic leader had stopped pressuring the oppressed follower to comply, would the follower have been justified to stay in the position?

Questions for Leaders

1. Is there anything this oppressed follower might have done to preserve his career with the company?
2. How would you have advised this oppressed follower if you were his mentor?
3. This case highlights a time when prevailing industry practices were corrupt and illegal (Avramenko & Boyd, 2013; Jones & Sirmans, 2019). What could an ethical leader have done in this environment?
4. Have you been in a situation where you believed you were the only person operating according to the rules? What pressure did this put on you to either conform to the group dynamic or stand out?

Case 13.2

The Testimonial

Many people consider education extremely necessary. Some say it is a necessity to the outcomes of having a good life, a stable career, and a safe place to call home. While I worked as a Language Development and Assessment Facilitator in a school, there were many ethical wrongdoings that hindered the success of the minority students, especially Hispanics. I couldn't believe the amount of wrongdoing against the students of minority in this well-known educational institution, nor I could grasp at the beginning of my job where to begin in hopes of making it right for these students and the overall institution. The main challenge was finding a way to tackle all of that. When I brought these issues to the department leader, she refused to change anything. I hate to use the term "racist", but that is how many in the department began to feel about her. She was a Caucasian woman, and many team members, including myself, heard her make racial comments about the Hispanic students. She would make comments about how they couldn't speak proper American, meaning English. She would make fun of how some of them looked and dressed.

Having experienced all this, it was not surprising that my proposals to help the minority students were never taken seriously. For instance, when I decided to talk to her about the option of assessing the new students in their mother language, which was Spanish, for the subjects of science, history, and mathematical skills (taking into account the importance of this assessments results, which would determine students grade placement at the school), she literally laughed in my face, told me to leave her office, and to work on "more important things". My proposal was based on the devastating assessment scores from the previous students over the past ten years or so. By taking this into account, the misunderstanding from students of this cohort in subjects like English was evident due to the fact that most of the students only have lived a few months in the United States.

Environment

Working in a toxic environment with a toxic leader is not an easy process to have to endure. This especially applies to a leader that is not willing to listen to other people's opinions, even if they know that others could be right. The work environment became frustrating and depressing. Trust was weakened, and I could tell many of my fellow team members were becoming unmotivated and stressed. We were there to help the students succeed. But it was nearly impossible to do so when our leader appeared to not care at all about that goal.

Coping and Outcome

There are many problems that one faces when encountering a situation where the leader with authority demonstrates unethical behavior, as influence causes employees to become fearful. Fear in the workplace weakens trust and communication. In the complex world of organizations, there are difficult challenges to overcome and one of the most challenging one is the person that supposed to be leading the organization is failing the entire team and organization with their lack of leadership and moral direction. The way our team coped was to wait it out and do the best we could for our students. We worked harder and longer hours, tutoring the Hispanic students and helping them as best we could. Finally, after a year, our leader left the position for another job. Some say she was let go due to enough complaints being reported against her. Either way, I am happy to report that our new leader is much more supportive of the minority students and has listened to our proposals to make sure that the Hispanic students are getting the help they need to succeed.

Reflection Journal

We recommend you keep a journal to reflect and write, using these questions to prompt your thinking.

1. The oppressed follower stated that the university was a "well-known institution". Do higher-profile institutions face a more difficult time when dealing with potentially high-profile issues?
2. West et al. (2021) defined racism at its simplest level as responding to people in demonstrably different ways based on race, and at a more advanced level as "intersecting individual, 'institutional, systemic, and cultural practices that perpetuate and maintain race-based hierarchies'" (Salter et al. as cited in West et al., 2021, p. 1137). Were the toxic leader's actions racist, according to either definition?
3. Many organizations faced employee criticism and turned an inward eye on the potential for racism within their organization. Did your organization face an internal or public reckoning? What were the results? Has anything changed fundamentally?

Basic Questions

1. What were the unethical behaviors of the toxic leader?
2. What coping mechanisms did the follower use?
3. What were the outcomes of the situation?

Advanced Questions

1. Do you see any difference between passive and overt demonstrations of discrimination?
2. What would make mocking a customer or employee's accent, language, or appearance evidence of discrimination?
3. How would you describe the culture of the organization?
4. Did the climate change after the toxic leader left?

Questions for Leaders

1. The oppressed follower hinted that the toxic leader might have been fired because of the complaints against her. Do employees have a right to know that their complaints have been heard and acted upon?
2. Multiple employees complained about the toxic leader's behaviors. What actions should the HR team have taken to address those complaints?
3. Does a supervisor have a duty to "listen to other people's opinions?" What are the implications for a supervisor who does not listen?
4. Griffith et al. (2007) conclude that addressing racism and oppression should be viewed as an ongoing process and not as a training objective. Does your organization take a process view toward diversity, equity, and inclusion?

Case 13.3

The Testimonial

Over the years, I developed a robust background in Public Relations, learning from a dynamic and brilliant leader who boasted a long work history in Corporate America. She was well versed in working with news media sources, developing effective communication campaigns, and exhibited a strong work ethic – often sending me texts and emails into the wee hours of the morning. Unfortunately, as much as she was a valuable contributor, she also exemplified a lack of ethics.

Environment

I discovered she was receiving compensation from us on a particular project and was also receiving compensation directly from the vendor for the same project. This was exceptionally difficult for me as I viewed her as both my mentor and my friend. On discovery of the double-dipping, I was forced to make a choice, to either look the other way, allowing the unethical behavior to continue, or do what was right and alert leadership. I chose the latter.

Outcome

The end outcome was leadership determining she would no longer provide services for the organization, which effectively ended a long-standing contracted business relationship. Not to mention the impact this had on her team as they not only were learning directly from her behaviour but they were also left in a precarious position of having to justify that behaviour. Had she known that her team was listening, watching, and modelling, she may have made better choices. Alas, she failed to appreciate or understand that her conduct had an influence on her follower's overall performance.

Given the many years of working with both effective and ineffective leaders, there has been much for me to glean from those experiences. As a result, I pledged to take hold of the positive attributes I had witnessed and abandon the practices that were toxic in nature. After I determined who I wanted to be as a leader, I then made a commitment to model that positive behavior consistently to enact a culture of business excellence and organizational leadership.

Reflection Journal

We recommend you keep a journal to reflect and write, using these questions to prompt your thinking.

1. The double-dipping in this situation had been going on for some time. Both organizations were receiving value from the leader's services. In fact, the follower reported that she exhibited a strong work ethic, routinely working late into the night. What was wrong with her taking compensation from both sources?
2. Receiving compensation from both sources was not illegal. Does your answer change if the organization did not have a code of conduct or ethical guidelines regarding conflicts of interest?
3. What feelings would you expect to have if you discovered that a mentor acted unethically and you needed to choose between loyalty to your mentor or adhering to your ethical standards?

Basic Questions

1. What unethical behavior did the follower discover?
2. Did the leader create a toxic environment?
3. What were the outcomes of the situation?

Advanced Questions

1. What message would have been sent to employees had the organization sanctioned the double-dipping?
2. Concerning the follower, what were the effects of upholding his ethical values?

Questions for Leaders

1. Is it possible to develop systems that prevent employees or contractors from acting unethically?
2. What systems can an organization put in place to help discourage unethical behavior?
3. Does your organization require employees to uphold a code of conduct?
4. Are your employees enculturated in your organization's values and expected ethical behaviors?

References

Avramenko, R., & Boyd, R. (2013). Subprime virtues: The moral dimensions of American housing and mortgage policy. *Perspectives on Politics, 11*(1), 111–131. https://doi.org/10.1017/S1537592712003672

Belal, A., Zeeshan, H., & Mohammed, A. (2021). Fire in the belly: The impact of despotic leadership on employees work-related outcomes in the hospitality setting. *International Journal of Contemporary Hospitality Management, 33*(10), 3564–3584. https://doi.org/10.1108/IJCHM-03-2021-0394

Bertland, A. (2009). Virtue ethics in business and the capabilities approach. *Journal of Business Ethics, 84*, 25–32. https://doi.org/10.1007/s10551-008-9686-3

Cote, R. (2018). Dark side leaders: Are their intentions benign or toxic? *Journal of Leadership, Accountability and Ethics, 15*(2), 42–65.

De Clercq, D., Fatima, T., & Jahanzeb, S. (2021). Ingratiating with despotic leaders to gain status: The role of power distance orientation and self-enhancement motive. *Journal of Business Ethics, 171*(1), 157–174. https://doi.org/10.1007/s10551-019-04368-5

Griffith, D. M., Mason, M., Yonas, M., Eng, E., Jeffries, V., Plihcik, S., & Parks, B. (2007). Dismantling institutional racism: Theory and action. *American Journal of Community Psychology, 39*(3–4), 381–392. https://doi.org/10.1007/s10464-007-9117-0

Jones, T., & Sirmans, G. S. (2019). Understanding subprime mortgage default. *Journal of Real Estate Literature, 27*(1), 27–52.

Riffut, J., & Nazahah, R. (2020). Exploring the effects of despotic leadership on employee engagement, employee trust and task performance. *Management Science Letters*. https://doi.org/10.5267/j.msl.2020.8.012

Shazia, N., Connie, Z., & Ameer, A. B. (2020). How despotic leadership jeopardizes employees' performance: The roles of quality of work life and work withdrawal. *Leadership & Organization Development Journal*, *42*(1), 1–16. https://doi.org/10.1108/LODJ-11-2019-0476

West, K., Greenland, K., & Laar, C. (2021). Implicit racism, colour blindness, and narrow definitions of discrimination: Why some white people prefer "all lives matter" to "Black lives matter". *British Journal of Social Psychology*, *60*(4), 1136–1153. https://doi.org/10.1111/bjso.12458

Zhou, X., Rasool, S. F., Yang, J., & Asghar, M. Z. (2021). Exploring the relationship between despotic leadership and job satisfaction: The role of self efficacy and leader–member exchange. *International Journal of Environmental Research and Public Health*, *18*(10). https://doi.org/10.3390/ijerph18105307

14 Coping Strategy Cases

Followers: Coping Strategies

Stress comes from an individual's psychological response to external job conditions (Berg & Karisen, 2013). As a subjective response, stress can be positive or negative. Positive stress can be stimulating and motivating, while negative stress indicates that the situation demands capabilities and resources beyond the individual's ability. "Coping strategies refer to the specific behavioral efforts that individuals employ to master, tolerate, reduce or minimize stressful events" (Folkman & Lazarus, 1980, as cited in Bhandarker & Rai, 2019). An individual's personality may directly relate to their coping styles (Hayes & Joseph, 2003, as cited in Ansar et al., 2021). Oppressed followers use active, passive, or adaptive coping strategies to deal with toxic leaders (Bhandarker & Rai, 2019).

Followers are more likely to use active coping strategies when the organization has an ethical climate. Active coping strategies include proactive and assertive measures such as reporting the toxic leader to higher authorities or confronting the toxic leader. In the study by Bhandarker and Rai (2019), followers complained to higher management, complained to the officers' association, left the organization, confronted the leader, or mobilized others against the leader.

Passive coping strategies include active and passive avoidance behaviors such as withholding effort and information, hiding problems and opportunities, disrupting operations, and undermining leaders or peers. Passive coping gives oppressed followers a sense of agency and control over unfair situations. Bhandarker and Rai (2019) reported that followers alienated and detached themselves, avoided interacting, stopped sharing business-related problems or opportunities, or minimized relations with the leader.

Followers who fear that the leader or peers will retaliate are more likely to use adaptive coping strategies. They might react by adapting their behavior to the situation, remaining silent, or ignoring the toxic behavior (Bhandarker & Rai, 2019). In their study, Bhandarker and Rai (2019) found that the followers' passive coping strategies included trying to maintain a

DOI: 10.4324/9781003202462-14

positive relationship with the leader, getting furious but intending to discuss issues later, or writing off the behavior as a bad phase that would pass. Some individuals cope by hiding their experiences from their coworkers to avoid feelings of shame (Bayramoğlu & Toksoy, 2017). Individuals might pray, give themselves pep talks, or meditate to diminish their stress levels (D'Cruz & Noronha, 2010).

Moos and Holahan (2003) suggested that coping styles or dispositions include problem-focused and avoidance coping. Some psychologists associate the Big-Five personality characteristics with task-oriented, emotion-oriented, and avoidance coping dispositions. They further connect these to depression and anxiety.

In a small study of ten organizations, D'Cruz and Noronha (2010) argued that organizational support is critical in helping employees cope successfully with a negative situation by separating the bully from the target. Unfortunately, that does not happen often, and followers who report their bully bosses do not receive organizational support. Instead, the followers claimed the organizations rejected the allegations and labeled them troublemakers, while the leaders intensified the bullying. Indeed, the organization often became a bully. D'Cruz and Noronha (2010) identified two typical phases that oppressed followers experienced. During the first phase, the oppressed follower is confused by a leader's negative behavior, gathers information, compares notes with peers, and assesses the severity of the situation. Eventually, the employee decides the leader is toxic and enters the second phase of engaging organizational options. See D'Cruz and Noronha (2010) for a detailed description of negative experiences with Human Resources departments reported by study participants. In most cases, human resource personnel avoided dealing with the oppressed followers and sided with the toxic leaders, causing the followers to feel doubly victimized. Peers often ostracized oppressed followers because they did not want to get caught up in the situation.

The following testimonials demonstrate follower coping strategies.

Case 14.1

The Testimonial

Only being two weeks into this job, I am able to cope okay for now because everyone, including the doctor, is nice to me since I am new, but I know as they become more comfortable with me, things will not be as easy. Of course, I don't want to make mistakes; I want to learn and not hurt any patients and entering a field that is completely new to me, the goal is to work hard and learn as much by practicing hands-on. However, what really occupies my mind most is to work harder, so I don't make mistakes in order to reduce the chances of being talked about negatively or being yelled at in front of others.

Aside from working harder as a coping strategy, I simply try to ignore my surroundings. Whenever I hear the doctor or the technicians talk about staff that is not present, I just keep myself busy and try not to listen. I never participate because I would never want someone to do that to me. Whenever someone is being chastised in front of me, I walk away because I know that person must feel embarrassed that others are watching; it is not a good feeling anyone wants to experience. I don't think I could submit a complaint because one of the managers there I believe has some connection to the doctor. The other manager I could possibly go to, but I don't feel comfortable doing so yet.

Outcome

Because of his consistent belittling and ridiculing in front of people, I believe it has caused the work environment to act similarly in ways where employees begin to gossip about everyone else behind their backs. I am brand new at the clinic, and I fear that when I am not there, others might be talking about me behind my back due to the fact that I have little experience in the veterinary field. I've never felt this way before, and I don't like having that fear. I accepted the job because I was thrilled to be given the opportunity to learn, but I think that is as far as invested I am in this job. I want to get my work experience out of the way (for my school) and once I get my required hours, I might resign or request fewer hours so I can continue learning and growing but having as little contact with the clinic as possible. Another thing I noticed, when I am not doing something correctly or it seems I am stressing out in front of clients, some of the managers there also tend to point it out in front of clients and other employees. I don't think it is appropriate to criticize someone in front of clients/customers. I think it would be ok in front of the staff if it is in a learning manner but not in front of customers.

Reflection Journal

We recommend you keep a journal to reflect and write, using these questions to prompt your thinking.

1. What did you notice in this case?

Basic Questions

1. Did the oppressed follower use active, passive, or adaptive coping strategies?
2. Did other followers support the employee or conspire with the toxic leader?
3. What were the outcomes of the coping strategies?

Advanced Questions

1. Were the coping strategies effective?
2. What coping strategies would you recommend?
3. Did the follower have a positive or a negative stress response?

Questions for Leaders

1. Is it acceptable to reprimand employees in front of other employees or customers?
2. How would you handle this situation if a new employee complained about someone who reported to you?
3. Would your organizational climate support an employee in actively coping with a toxic leader?

Case 14.2

The Testimonial

The events I experienced with the toxic leader continued until I left, but there were a few different ways in which I was able to cope during that time. I was given the ability to work from home for my position, and though it did not alleviate all of the toxic behaviors and experiences, it did allow me to distance myself from it when needed. I was able to work at my own pace and still produce exceptional results. Not being in an office with the toxic leader also provided the opportunity to detach because I was able to keep my work and personal life separate. Not having them looking over my shoulder every day, or listening to my phone calls and making comments, or being available at any time to discuss non-work-related matters really helped in coping with the experience.

Outcome

Towards the end of my time in that organization, changes were started because of previous events that showed potential for improvements.

A coworker had quit and filed a complaint with the Executive Board about the unfair and discriminatory practices of the leader. The process then involved lawyers and interviews of myself and the other employees in determining the credibility and severity of the situation. I was able to voice all of my concerns in a confidential format but was unable to receive any updates on what the outcome would be. It was not until the end that I was informed that the organization hired an outside firm to act as a human resources department. What I found strange, though, was that towards the end of my time there, I attempted to contact the person hired by the organization and never heard back. I reached out to the president of the board and never heard from them either. It added to the stress and anxiety of the job that the leadership that was supposed to be monitoring the toxic leadership of my boss was not accountable or reachable.

Toxic work environments can be determinantal to not only the emotional but physical and mental health of an employee. In the situation I experienced, I had severe anxiety, a loss of confidence in my work abilities, and felt very isolated because of my work. The outcome was that I was finally able to leave the organization, which, over time, provided me with the chance to recover from the emotional berating and toxic behavior inflicted by the toxic leadership I experienced. Prior to the job, I had confidence in organizational accountability and believed that if certain lines were crossed in the workplace, it would have consequences. Unfortunately, my time at the organization proved otherwise, as my health and age were both commented on throughout my time there. The inconsistency and toxic behaviors were what pushed me to find a new job.

Had it not been for the unique circumstances that resulted in working from home for a majority of my time with the organization, the opportunities to cope with and distance from the toxic leadership and work environment would not have been available, and the experiences would most likely have been more severe. It became apparent in this organization that the toxic behaviors that the leadership expressed went unchecked for a long time by the Executive Board and could have become more extreme as a result. The experiences with this organization and toxic leadership gave guidance for what to look out for in future jobs or leadership situations, as well as what not to do as a leader.

Reflection Journal

We recommend you keep a journal to reflect and write, using these questions to prompt your thinking.

1. What did you notice in this case?

2. The oppressed follower noted that a previous employee resigned and filed a complaint with the executive board. Is it possible that the complaint held more weight because the person quit?

Basic Questions

1. Did the oppressed follower use active, passive, or adaptive coping strategies?
2. Did other followers support the employee or conspire with the toxic leader?
3. What were the outcomes of the coping strategies?

Advanced Questions

1. Were the coping strategies effective?
2. What coping strategies would you recommend?
3. Did the follower have a positive or a negative stress response?

Questions for Leaders

1. Would you consider this a successful resolution?
2. In what ways did the organization support or fail the oppressed followers?
3. The employee mentioned the feelings of stress over not knowing what was happening with the situation. What could the employer do to help employees cope with a pending human resource resolution?

Case 14.3

The Testimonial

Coping with toxic leadership can be emotionally draining and exhausting. The way I have been handling toxic leadership is by accepting that I am not the problem. I am still very committed to doing my job to the best of my ability, so my boss does not have a reason to target me. Also, I have a journal where I document every negative conversation, text message, or comment that she says. I keep a strong mentality and remind myself that her perception of me is not who I am.

Finally, I have written four letters of complaint to human resources in the past two years. I have noted that no action takes place and that the letters are filed just for the record. Now, I do not waste my time writing complaints because I see that nothing changes or improves. Currently, she still holds her position. No corrective action has taken place to fix the issue by senior management, although almost all her employees have complained about her toxic leadership. The rumor is she has good connections with headquarters, so she is here to stay for a long while.

Outcome

The end outcome of her toxic leadership is high employee turnover and waste of resources. Almost every three months, an employee resigns, and we have to hire and train new employees. Overall, toxic leadership often hinders productivity and innovation, increases employee dissatisfaction, causes conflict, and destroys employee morale.

Reflection Journal

We recommend you keep a journal to reflect and write, using these questions to prompt your thinking.

1. What did you notice in this case?
2. As with many toxic situations, complaints to human resources do not result in positive changes for the oppressed followers. Given the research on the organizational outcomes of toxic leadership, why do you think that human resource departments have a difficult time dealing with toxic leaders?

Basic Questions

1. Did the oppressed follower use active, passive, or adaptive coping strategies?
2. Did other followers support the employee or conspire with the toxic leader?
3. What were the outcomes of the coping strategies?

Advanced Questions

1. Were the coping strategies effective?
2. What coping strategies would you recommend?
3. Did the follower have a positive or a negative stress response?

Questions for Leaders

1. Is it a good idea for employees to keep a diary or log of any issues with their supervisors?

2. Would you advise the oppressed follower to continue to log complaints with human resources?
3. The toxic supervisor supposedly has "good connections with headquarters". Does this make a difference in how the organization treats its followers?
4. How would you proceed if the employee reached out to you for mentorship?

References

Ansar, A., Ekowati, D., & Suhariadi, F. (2021). Individual psychological distance: A leadership task to assess and cope with invisible change [individual psychological distance and leadership]. *The Journal of Management Development*, *40*(3), 168–189. https://doi.org/10.1108/JMD-09-2020-0304

Bayramoğlu, M. M., & Toksoy, D. (2017). Leadership and bullying in the forestry organization of turkey. *BioMed Research International*, *11*. https://doi.org/10.1155/2017/9454682

Berg, M. E., & Karlsen, J. T. (2013). Managing stress in projects using coaching leadership tools. *Engineering Management Journal*, *25*(4), 52–61.

Bhandarker, A., & Rai, S. (2019). Toxic leadership: Emotional distress and coping strategy. *International Journal of Organization Theory and Behavior*, *22*(1), 65–78. https://doi.org/10.1108/IJOTB-03-2018-0027

D'Cruz, P., & Noronha, E. (2010). The exit coping response to workplace bullying: The contribution of inclusivist and exclusivist HRM strategies. *Employee Relations*, *32*(2), 102–120. https://doi.org/10.1108/01425451011010078

Moos, R. H., & Holahan, C. J. (2003). Dispositional and contextual perspectives on coping: Toward an integrative framework: Coping (part 2-measurement). *Journal of Clinical Psychology*, *59*(12), 1387–1403.

15 Conclusion

Summary

Dozens of scholars have researched and written about forms of toxic leadership, including other descriptors such as bad leadership, destructive leadership, the shadow side of leadership, dark leadership, and unethical leadership. We attempted to unify those various strands of research on toxic leadership and related concepts. We discussed the most salient aspects of the various contributions in bringing these ideas together. Nevertheless, in such a comprehensive endeavor, we are sure to have missed important contributions. We hope to become aware of these contributions for future editions.

We gave special attention to the concept of power, which seems central to toxic leader behavior. We also covered personality disorders, followers, and organizational culture and climate. We would have liked to have discussed other important issues, such as the relationships between toxic leadership and followers of different ages, gender, race, and other demographics. Some followers discussed the perceived benefits of working under toxic leaders, which is a topic for further inquiry.

In this edition, we presented our typology of toxic leaders, which included six types: aberrant toxic leaders, leaders who abuse their power, egocentric toxic leaders, leaders who demonstrate emotional dysregulation, and spectacularly ineffective toxic leaders. These archetypes capture many of the toxic leadership characteristics from many other models. However, we derived our types from analyzing the cases of 130 followers. That analysis resulted in our closed and open systems models of toxic leadership, which describe the relationships between toxic leaders, oppressed followers, the organization, and other stakeholders.

Directions for Future Inquiry

Our investigation has uncovered as many questions as answers. We hope to continue to explore the toxic leadership landscape; to further define, develop, and categorize toxic leader archetypes; and refine the open systems

DOI: 10.4324/9781003202462-15

model of toxic leadership to be useful for organizational interventions. Some questions for ongoing inquiry:

1. Are toxic leaders aware that followers perceive them as toxic?
2. Would toxic leaders agree with their followers' perspectives?
3. Are toxic leaders aware of the effects they have on followers?
4. Are toxic leaders aware of their effect on organizational outcomes?
5. What are the most effective organizational interventions to stop toxic leadership?
6. What are the most effective external interventions that might help (e.g., litigation, social media pressure)
7. Which organizational climates are most likely to create or perpetuate toxic leadership?
8. What are the most effective actions that allies can take to help oppressed followers?
9. What should a leader do when suspecting a subordinate is a toxic leader?
10. Do leaders without positional power exhibit toxic leadership?

ToxicLeaderStory.com

Stories are a powerful means of communication. They help us to connect and relate. Hopefully, sharing our stories can help us heal. We invite you to share your toxic leader stories at https://toxicleaderstory.com. You can choose to remain anonymous, and we provide a template to help you. By sharing your story, you might be helping others who are going through similar situations.

Future Editions

We encountered many ups and downs that are probably not unique to our writing and collaboration processes as we wrote this book. One concern is that we have not said everything we want or need to say about the topic. At some point, though, we have to stop and say, "This is good enough for now; save the rest for the sequel!"

To this end, we will refine our ideas and incorporate additional lines of inquiry into future editions. We intend to develop new chapters on age, gender, race, and other demographics. We will also provide new cases covering unique perspectives, demographics, and voices. Finally, we hope to include tools for instructors such as guides related to toxic leadership in movies and literature and recommended curriculum.

Author Biographies

Dr. Steven M. Walker

Dr. Steven M. Walker holds a PhD degree in Leadership Studies from Gonzaga University in Spokane, Washington. His primary interests have been in toxic leadership, crisis leadership, leadership for sustainability, complex adaptive leadership, and leadership during economic recessions. His dissertation research was on the Great Recession of 2008 and, as a breaking point in the economic system, its impact on the psyche and behavior of organizational leaders. He has presented research across the United States, Canada, Spain, and Belgium. Dr. Walker currently resides in San Diego, California, with his son where they enjoy basketball, surfing, and hiking in their spare time.

Dr. Daryl V. Watkins

Dr. Watkins is an educator and US Navy Combat Veteran with a background in higher education, public transportation, information technology management, and military aviation.

A professor of leadership at Embry-Riddle Aeronautical University, he teaches courses in strategic leadership, coaching and mentoring, critical thinking, and transformation and change. He researches leadership topics such as leading in complex environments, toxic leadership, and developing leaders. Dr. Watkins has taught, facilitated workshops, and presented research in Australia, Belgium, Mexico, Spain, India, Singapore, Japan, and Trinidad and Tobago. He was recognized as the Teacher of the Year by the Association for College Business Schools and Programs.

Dr. Watkins held positions as Interim Dean, Associate Dean, Assistant Dean, Department Chair, and Program Chair within the Embry-Riddle Worldwide College of Business. Before joining ERAU in 2010, Dr. Watkins was an Operations Manager and General Manager of two toll roads in Orange County, California. He also flew F/A 18 Hornets off the aircraft carrier, USS *Midway*, during Operation Desert Storm.

He is CEO and co-founder of LDRC, a leadership development and coaching firm located in Orange County, California. He holds certifications in coaching, career coaching, CliftonStrengths coaching, project management, organization development, mediation, and grant writing. He has also served multiple years as an examiner for the Malcolm Baldrige National Quality Award.

Dr. Watkins lives in Orange, California, with his wife of 27 years, Dr. Nancy Watkins. They have three adult children. He enjoys Los Angeles Dodgers baseball, single-malt Scotch whiskeys, and cavorting with dogs, friends, and Jeeps in the red rocks of Sedona, Arizona.

Index

Aasland, M.S. 13
aberrant behavior cases 61–73
aberrant behaviors 46, 52, 61
abuse of power 15, 17, 46, 48, 52, 74, 77, 79
abuse of power cases 74–86
abusive behaviors 11, 26–27, 76, 81, 85
abusive supervisors 78, 82, 84
adaptive coping strategies 128, 131, 133–134
ADHD 96
affective disorders 105
Alqurashi, S. 23
Ammons, D.L. 36–37, 39–40
Anjum, A. 3, 5, 49, 59
Ansar, A. 128, 135
anti-social personality disorder 18, 20
apathy 39, 47, 49, 51, 95
archetypes 51, 136
arrogance 12–13, 20, 22, 62
Asghar, M.Z. 127
Aubé, C. 26, 30
Avolio, B.J. 5
Avramenko, R. 120–121, 126
Ayub, N. 22–23

Babiak, P. 13, 24
bad leadership 5, 9–11, 13–14, 23, 136
Bai, Y. 60, 95
Baloyi, G.T. 52, 59, 74, 86
Bamel, U.K. 39–40
Barbuti, M. 105
Barker, M. 30
Bartone, P.T. 23
Bayramoğlu, M.M. 135
behaviors: bad 58, 79, 98; collective 47, 49, 51; destructive 7, 9; destructive leader 9, 28; egocentric 50, 87, 89; ineffective leader 46, 48, 50; toxic leader's 25, 67, 69, 72, 112, 124; unethical leader 53–54, 118
Belal, A. 118, 126
Berg, M.E. 135
Bertland, A. 121, 126
Bhandarker, A. 128, 135
bias 55–56, 58, 85
blaming 20, 53, 106
bonds 27, 29, 33, 47
borderline personality disorder 18, 20–21, 96
Boyd, R. 120–121, 126
Brancati, G.E. 96, 105
Brochet, F. 37, 39–40
Broome, M. 105
Brough, P. 31
Brouwers, M. 53, 60, 106, 117
bullying 11–14, 20, 27, 30, 53, 118, 129, 135
Burch, G. 13, 18, 24
Burns, W.A. 4–5, 38, 53–54, 59

Camgöz, S.M. 30, 59
Carsten, M.K. 28–29
Carton, A.M. 117
Castro, S. 30
Cavaiola, A.A. 23
Cheng, M.Y. 86
Chimpanzee politics 17
climate 32, 34–35, 39, 44, 56, 65, 69, 78–79, 85, 89, 121; psychological 35, 40–41
coaching 36, 138–139
coercive power 15–17
compassion ix, 22, 29, 59, 88, 102, 105
compliance 21, 38, 62
conflict 23, 78, 134
Conrad, D. 11, 13
Cooper, C.L. 13, 30

coping 29–30, 64, 66, 75, 78, 80, 83, 93, 95, 97, 99–100, 102, 131, 133, 135
coping mechanisms 71–72, 78, 108–109, 116, 124
coping strategies x, 27, 49, 57, 65, 98, 101, 104, 128, 130–131, 133–135
coping strategy cases 128–135
Costabile 43
Cote, R. 26, 29, 38, 40, 51, 53, 59, 118, 126
Cotugno, B. 105
counterproductive work behavior (CWB) 23, 26, 59, 105
COVID-19 pandemic 63
creativity 53, 59–60, 87, 95, 118
culture 4–5, 32–42, 51–52, 54, 56, 61, 65, 67, 70, 74, 90, 92, 124–125; adaptive 36; national 33; strong 36–37; weak 36–37, 40
CWB (counterproductive work behavior) 23, 26, 59, 105

Daft, R. 3, 5, 53, 59
Daly, K. 31
dark leadership 18, 136
D'Cruz, P. 129, 135
definition 4, 7, 9–11, 13, 18, 123
Denney, V.P. 111, 117
destructive leadership 8–9, 14, 30–31, 59, 136; defined 8
development 35, 38, 43, 59, 93, 105
de Vries, R. 26, 29, 50, 60
diagnostic 18, 23, 73
Dillard, J.E. 27, 30
disciplinary action 2, 80, 83
disorder 19, 22
Dobbs, J.M. 26, 29, 49, 53, 59, 106, 116
Dollard, M.F. 29
dominance hierarchy placement 16
DSM 18–21, 23, 73
Duffy, M. 6

egocentric cases 87–95
Einarsen, S. 8, 11, 13
Ekmekci, Ö. T. 30, 59
Ekowati, D. 135
emotional dysregulation 46, 48, 53, 96, 101, 105, 109, 136
emotional dysregulation cases 97–105
emotional exhaustion 27, 54, 59, 118
emotional intelligence 22, 53, 60, 96, 100–101, 107
emotional outbursts 37, 68, 97, 102
emotions, negative 53–54, 97
empathy, lack of 52, 62–63, 70
employee morale 111, 134
Eng, E. 126
Epitropaki, O. 28–29
Eyden, J. 105

Faragher, B. 13
Fatima, T. 126
Fisher, K. 13, 18, 23
Fitzgibbons, K.A. 39–40
follower coping strategies 47, 49, 129
followers 2–5, 7–12, 15–18, 25–32, 39, 44, 47–57, 63–68, 92, 101, 109–110, 112, 116, 118, 125–126, 128–129, 133–137
Foresman, S. 30
Fors Brandebo, M. 10–11, 13
Friedman, H. 26, 29, 53, 59, 96, 105

Gabriel, J. 26, 29, 49, 53, 59, 96, 105
Gagné, M. 116
Gallos, J.V. 25, 29
Gallus, J.A. 25, 29
Gardner, W.L. 5
gender 5, 19, 38, 42, 75, 136–137
Gerhardt, M. 24
Gerstein, M. 26, 29, 53, 59, 96, 105
Glick, W.H. 35, 40
Goldman, A. 18, 23
Gonçalves, H. 14
Graen, G.B. 4–5
Grashow, A. 5
Greenleaf, R. 4–5
Griffith, D.M. 124, 126
Grijalva, E. 22–23
Guinan, P. 31
Gupta, G. 29

de Haan, E. 13, 18, 23
Hackman, J.R. 115
Hamblin, R.L. 5
Han, G.H. 60
Hantouche, E.G. 105
Hare, R. 13, 24
Harms, P.D. 60
Hartog, D.N. 23
Harvey, P. 27, 29
Haslam, S.A. 60, 95
Heifetz, R.A. 4–5
von Hellman, B. 42
Henderson, M. 30
Henle, C. 6
Hersey, P. 4–5
Heskett, J.L. 36, 41

Hickman, G. 3, 5, 7, 13
Hinshaw, S. 43, 60
Hochwarter, W. 29
Hoel, H. 11, 13, 28, 30
Hofstede, G. 32–34, 40–41
Hogan, J 18, 24
Hogan, R. 18, 24
Holahan, C.J. 129, 135
Holloway, E. 25, 30
De Hoogh, A.H.B. 22–23
human resource management 29, 59–60, 95, 105, 117
human resources 38–39, 58, 66, 72, 110, 112, 129, 133–135
Hunter, S. 31
Hyde 63

in-crowd 93
ineffective leadership 12, 106–109, 112, 114
ineffective leadership cases 107–117
in-group 38, 85–86, 91, 94

Jahanzeb, S. 126
Jeffries, V. 126
Jehn, K. 23
Jin, Z. 30
job satisfaction 8, 13–14, 24, 26, 53, 60, 106, 117, 127
Johnsen, B.H. 23
Johnson, S.M. 39
Jones, A.P. 39, 41
Jones, T. 120, 126

Kacmar, C. 29
Kaiser, R.B. 18, 24
Kapuchinski, S. 19, 24
Karisen, J.T. 135
Kellerman, B. 5, 7, 9–11, 13, 29–30
Kendrick, K. 26, 30, 49, 52
Kennedy, A.A. 36, 40
Khoo, H. 13, 18, 24
Kipnis, D. 28, 30
Kotter, J.P. 36, 41
Krasikova, D.V. 8–9, 12, 13
Kusy, M. 25, 30

Laar, C. 127
Laberg, J.C. 23
Lambert, L. 6
Larsson, G. 13
Lavender, N.J. 23
leaders 2–5, 7–12, 15–18, 22–23, 25–26, 28–30, 34–36, 38–39, 43–47, 50–58, 65–67, 69–72, 74, 78–80, 85, 88–95, 101–104, 120–129, 131–134, 136–137; abusive 26–27, 78; corrupt 54, 118; egocentric 53, 87, 89–90, 92; ineffective 9, 109, 114–116, 125; narcissistic 23, 60, 68, 89; organizational 36, 40, 56, 61, 138; strong 8, 77, 79, 115
leadership 3–6, 9–14, 16–18, 22–24, 29, 35, 44–46, 53, 59–60, 71, 81–82, 85–86, 106–107, 117–118, 125–126, 132, 135–136, 138; despotic 60, 118, 126–127
leadership theory 6, 17, 24
LeBreton, J.M. 13
Lewicki, R.J. 15, 17
Leyman, H. 28, 30
Li, X. 27, 30
Liao, Z. 30
Linsky, M. 5
Lipman-Blumen, J. 3, 5–7, 12, 13, 25, 30
Lubit, R.H. 20, 22, 24

Maamari, B.E. 53, 60
Maccoby, M. 52, 60
Machiavellianism 13, 18
Majdalani, J.F. 53, 60
Marwaha, S. 96, 105
Mason, M. 126
Mathieu, C. 13, 18, 24
Matos, K. 51, 53, 87, 95
McCarthy, P. 30
McGreal, S.A. 22–24
Metin-Orta, I. 27, 30
micromanaging 27, 46, 48, 53, 55, 74, 106, 114
Millette, V. 116
Ming, X. 5, 59
Minkov, M. 33, 40–41
model of toxic leadership 5, 54, 137
Mohammed, A. 126
Mohiuddin, Z. 26, 30, 51, 60
Moos, R.H. 129, 135
moral corruption cases 118–127
Moran, E.T. 34, 41
Moreira, J.M. 14

Namnyak, M. 104–105
narcissism 13, 18, 22–24, 27, 46, 48, 60–61, 68, 72
narcissistic personality disorder 18, 21–22, 61–62, 67
Naseer, S. 60, 95

Nash, S. 11, 13
Nazahah, R. 126
Neuijen, B. 40
Neumann, C. 13, 24
Nevicka, B. 23
Newman, D.A. 22–23
Nielsen, M.B. 11–12, 14
Nilsson, S. 13
Nonaka, I. 104–105
Noronha, E. 129, 135
Nusair, D. 60

Oldham, G.R. 115
Ong, C.W. 60
oppressed followers 38, 54–58, 63–65, 67, 78–79, 81–82, 84–85, 91, 94, 101, 104, 109, 111–112, 121, 123–124, 128–129, 133–137
organizational climate 11–12, 32, 34–35, 39–41, 47, 49, 51, 54, 59–60, 109, 118
organizational culture 7–8, 18, 29, 32–37, 39–41, 84, 91, 105, 109, 111, 121
organizational environment 18, 54, 63, 66, 68, 70, 92, 119
organizational outcomes 47–49, 59, 62, 67, 69, 76, 112, 134, 137; negative 3, 26, 37
organizational psychology 13, 23, 29
Ostroff, C. 41
outcomes 9–11, 14–15, 44, 46–47, 50–51, 55–56, 78, 84–85, 89–91, 100–101, 103–104, 106–111, 115–116, 122–126, 130–134
out-groups 38, 85–86, 91

Padilla, A. 31
Pallucchini, A. 105
Paltu, A. 53, 60, 106, 117
paranoia 46, 48, 61, 72
paranoid personality disorder 18–20, 61–62, 69
Pelletier, K.L. 8, 11–12, 14
performance 30, 37, 41–42, 45, 60, 66, 115–116, 125, 127
Pittinsky, T.L. 60
Plihcik, S. 126
Plonien, C. 11–12, 14
polarity 69, 76, 94, 105, 111
power 4–5, 10, 12, 15–17, 21, 23, 25–30, 46, 48, 52, 57–58, 74, 76–77, 79–81, 136; positional 12, 16, 56, 100, 137
power cases 74–86
psychopathy 13, 18

Qian, J. 30

race 5, 42, 123, 136–137
Rai, S. 128, 135
Raskin, R. 52, 60
Rasool, G. 5, 52–54, 59–60, 87, 95, 127
Rayner, C. 28, 30
Reed, G.E. 7, 12, 14
reflexive loop 55–56
ridiculing 52, 107, 130
Riffut, J. 126
Roberts, R. 60
Roque 10–11, 13–14
Rosenthal, S.A. 60
Rost, J. 6
Rousseau, V. 26, 30

Salter 123
Sampson, E.L. 105
Sanders, G. 40
Sarros, J. 13, 23
Saunders, D.M. 17
Schaffer, H.R. 87
Schein, E.H. 32, 34–36, 39, 41
Schiavi, E. 105
Schilling, J. 9, 12, 14
Schmidt, S. 30, 53, 60, 106, 117
Schneider, B. 32, 39, 41
Schriesheim, C. 28, 30
Schwartz 10
Schyns, B. 9, 12, 14, 22–24
Sen, Amartya 121
shadows ix, 13, 23–24, 58
Sheehan, M. 28, 30
Shemla, M. 60, 95
Siddiqi, A.F. 5, 59
Singh, S.P. 105
Skogstad, A. 13
Snook, S.A. 23
social psychology 41, 60, 86, 127
Sottolano, D. 31
Sparks, K. 30
Steele, J.P. 8, 12, 14
Stockholm syndrome 104–105
Stokes, P. 40
Stoner, J. 29
Suhariadi, F. 135
supervision, abusive 6, 29–30, 60, 95
supervisor, toxic 101, 109, 113, 135
Syed, F. 60, 95
Szekely, R. 105

Tajfel, H. 41, 85–86
Tepper, B. 5–8, 14
Terry, H. 52, 60
Thoroughgood, C. 28, 31
Toal, M. 105
Toksoy, D. 135
toxic behaviors 25–27, 40, 45, 47–48, 53, 56–58, 70, 76, 81, 106–107, 128, 131–132
toxic leader archetypes 51, 136
toxic leader behaviors 46–47, 49, 136
toxic leaders x, 5–8, 25–29, 37–40, 42–43, 45–48, 50–51, 53–58, 60–61, 64–67, 69–71, 103–104, 112, 116, 121–122, 124, 128–129, 131, 133–134, 136–137
toxic leadership ix–x, 3, 5, 7–8, 14–15, 25–32, 39–40, 42–43, 45–46, 51–52, 54–56, 58–61, 70–71, 74, 117, 132–138
toxic protectors 25
traits 46, 52, 96, 98, 100; narcissistic 68; negative 50, 52; positive leadership 52; toxic 20, 22, 53
transformational leadership 5, 13, 24
trust 15–16, 51, 55. 58, 67, 70–71, 88, 102–103, 106, 113, 115, 119, 122–123
Tuckey, M.R. 29
Tufton, N. 105
Turner, J.C. 38, 41, 85–86
turnover intentions 27, 60, 117

Uhl-Bien, M. 4–5, 28–29
unethical behavior 20, 47, 51, 121, 123–126

van Driel, M. 29
victims 30, 57, 80, 104
Volkwein, J.F. 34, 41

De Waal, F. 16–17
Walker, S.M. 43, 138
Wallace, J. 39, 41
Walsh, B.M. 29
Watkins, D.V. 111, 117, 138–139
Webster, V. 27, 31
Wegge, J. 49, 52–53, 60, 87, 95
Whicker, M. 14
Wilkinson, I. 30
Willsie, S. 29
Wolke, D. 105
Woodman, T. 60

Al-Yafi, W. 23
Yammarino, F. 30
Yang, J. 127
Yasharoff, H. 42, 60
Yonas, M. 126
Yukl, G. 28, 31

Zeeshan, H. 126
Zeitschrift 95
Zhou, X. 118, 127
Zwerdling, D. 43

Made in the USA
Las Vegas, NV
19 September 2026

dfca0be0-fe2c-4346-bf04-09a909d32104R02